From Incarnation to Re-Incarnation

Also from Westphalia Press

westphaliapress.org

From Incarnation to Re-Incarnation

by Richard Ingalese
and
Isabella Ingalese

WESTPHALIA PRESS
An imprint of Policy Studies Organization

From
Incarnation to Re-incarnation

BY
RICHARD INGALESE
AND
ISABELLA INGALESE

Revised Edition

The Occult Book Concern
PUBLISHERS
9 TO 15 MURRAY STREET
NEW YORK CITY

WATKINS PRESS
NEW YORK

TO STUDENTS OF TRUTH EVERYWHERE

*"New occasions teach new duties: Time
    makes ancient good uncouth;
They must upward still, and onward, who
    would keep abreast of Truth;
Lo, before us gleam her camp-fires! we
    ourselves must Pilgrims be,
Launch our Mayflower, and steer boldly
    through the desperate winter sea,
Nor attempt the Future's portals with the
    Past's blood rusted key."*

The Present Crisis—LOWELL.

PREFACE

In taking up a new study, or in extending an old one, a person is frequently confronted with views which may not harmonize with his preconceptions. In this book, originally issued as a course of lectures, there is much which disagrees with the now accepted theological, often mistakenly called "religious," social and scientific opinions and theories. A liberal and progressive man, without bias, will examine new ideas before passing judgment upon them. We therefore expect each student to withhold judgment until the end of the Course and until he is satisfied that he understands the presentation of the Occult Philosophy.

The Course naturally divides itself into two parts, Anthropology and Cosmogony. The former, being more within the realm of common knowledge and experience, will naturally appeal more quickly to the general reader than will the latter. It must be admitted, however, that modern science is sadly at sea concerning Cosmogony, since it offers several conflicting theories concerning the same. Most religionists have abandoned the Cosmogony of Genesis as it is commonly interpreted and understood. In the absence, therefore, of what the world usually regards as authoritative teachings on the subject, the Cosmogony of Occultism may supply at least a working hypothesis which is both as scientific and philosophic as is that offered by either modern science or religion.

To those who can accept the Anthropology herein contained, but not the Cosmogony, we—like Galileo, who attempted to teach the construction and order of the Universe to the learned men of his time—can but assert the truth, praying the unconvinced reader, as he did the Grand Duke, "to consider it as mere poetry, or as a dream; nevertheless, as the poets sometimes set value upon their fancies, so I likewise have a certain esteem for this my novelty."

We recommend the student to observe the following method of study as far as possible: Read slowly an entire lecture and then read all references cited in the lecture. Afterward re-read the entire lecture in view of such side lights. Divide the lecture into seven or several portions, and read one portion each day; and meditate upon the portion read. Those who will observe this suggestion will find much more in the Course than will those who do not.

This Course is intended to act as a door through which the man or mind enters the current of Philosophic Truth in the Divine Consciousness, which will Itself instruct and illumine each individual mind according to its desire and ability to receive enlightenment.

The citation to pages in "The History and Power of Mind" refer to the paging of the second edition. By adding (1) to the pages cited between 31 and 119 inclusive, and (2) to all pages between 120 and 284 inclusive, the same reference may be found in the first edition. In both editions the paging is the same between 1 and 30.

There is nothing original on the part of the undersigned in the Philosophy set forth in this Course. Being true, it has always existed. If it appeals to you as true, accept it, and if you accept it, solemnly resolve to live up to it. If it does not appeal to you as true, then you at least have the satisfaction of knowing that you have become acquainted with the Oldest Philosophy in the World, and one which has been handed down literally from time immemorial.

We hold ourselves responsible for the correct presentation of the Philosophy as it was taught to us, and assert that our experiences and observations during a long period of study of Occultism—fifteen and thirty years respectively—verify its truth.

R. I. and I. I.

New York City,
    February 1st, 1904.

PREFACE TO THE SECOND EDITION.

The demand for another printing of this book gives us an opportunity to correct many errors which crept into the first edition. These lectures were written as a correspondence course for students residing in all parts of the world, and were issued at the rate of one chapter a week. To write a chapter, have it printed, to mail it and to answer questions concerning it, proved more laborious and exacting than was anticipated. This labor was in addition to our other duties of teaching, corresponding and healing, which were a part of our mission at that time. Under such strenuous circumstances many errors inadvertently found place in the original lectures and when the book was immediately published from the same type, the errors were incorporated in the text. The more vital ones were subsequently corrected for many students, and now we have the pleasure of doing the same duty for the Public.

R. I. and I. I.

San Jose, California,
July 1st, 1907.

CONTENTS.

CONTENTS

FROM INCARNATION TO RE-INCARNATION.

LECTURE ONE.

THE RELATION OF SEX.

Before the beginning of our Cosmic Day, and before "God created the heavens and the earth," the Father-Mother, the Creating and the Fructifying, the Giving and the Receiving, the Positive and Negative, the Male and Female aspects of the Universal Principle existed.

While the darkness of the Cosmic Night prevailed throughout the Universe, and while the Elohim or Planetary Spirits were sub-consciously resting in the bosom of the Infinite, God said: "Let there be light," and the Positive Divine Force went instantly forth from the great Cosmic Heart into the silent, negative Ether; vibration began, and the first morning of our Cosmic Day was born.[1]

When our World was in a vaporous condition—an irregular, shapeless mass of burning gases—the Universal Principle called forth from the Ether, in which all things latently reposed, the different elements which combined and solidified and produced

---

[1] The History and Power of Mind, pp. 36-43; 101-105.

the mineral kingdom of our Earth. And after her creation was completed and her orbit in the heavens established, for ages she still remained in a negative condition, receptive only to the restless, surging Father Force—the sea—which covered, magnetized, enriched, and made it possible for her to "bring forth" and bear upon her capacious bosom the vegetable and animal creations which she had conceived in the darkness and the silence.

Then again was Divine Will put into operation, and the waters were "gathered together unto one place," in order that the dry land—the Mother Earth—should appear and "bring forth." And when she had clothed herself in beautiful verdure she concealed beneath her green mantle the precious stones and rich minerals which had been created within her in the beginning of her existence. But nothing in all the Universe was made in vain, and it was not intended by the Universal Principle that these mineral riches should be thus and forever hidden. They, with all the various fauna and flora, were placed in readiness to be made subject to the wills of the Sons of God when they should come and desire to appropriate them.

As many more ages as Mother Earth had lain dormant under the sea did she require to evolve from her animal kingdom a form with brain of sufficient vibratory power to enable it to receive from the Universal Principle the Divine Spark which would lead and enlighten it throughout the ages to come. And when this triumph had been gained and animal man stood erect and walked upon two feet instead of four, he knew very little about himself and nothing about his source.

But, "One day is with the Lord as a thousand years and a thousand years as one day," and, after what would seem to men of the present age an almost interminable length of time, the law of Evolution, which is God's will operating in every living thing, brought to the Earth and to each of her animal men a subjective mind or soul to work out a double purpose:[1] First, to gain for itself greater strength and power by contacting with a material world of a lower rate of vibration than its own; and, second, to subject animal man and to raise him to a higher point of development.

When these subjective minds or souls first came to Earth they knew nothing of sex or of things sensory or sensual. But each had indeed been created in the image of God and was a part of the Father-Mother Principle; therefore each of the subjective minds possessed both a positive and a negative side to its nature.

In the realm where these minds had dwelt before coming to earth[2] this complexity in each had caused no inharmonious conditions, since there had been no trials to endure and no temptations to resist. Exist-

[1] The History and Power of Mind, pp. 64-72.

[2] The former as well as the future planetary homes of the soul will be discussed in the proposed course "Cosmogony and Evolution."

ence there had been a blissful, beautiful dream. But when these Sons of God came to this world and "saw the daughters of men," the animal forms which had been raised to receive them for their lords, each mind was forced to make its selection, and it was then that the sex question, with all its ramifications and mystifications, arose.

Acting according to its natural tendencies, the positive part of each of these subjective minds was attracted toward the female animal form, while the negative part of each mind, by reason of its nature, was attracted toward the male animal form. This caused dissention through jealousy, and war was declared in the heaven of each individual mind. Then came the first divorce ever granted upon this earth, and God gave one to each of Its Sons. It came through the Courts of Evolutionary Law, of which the divorce courts of the present day are but remote ramifications.

These first divorces, like those of the present day, were given for the purpose of permitting each Son of God to work out his salvation in his own way; in other words, to give him free will. And since there were more animal forms than there were Sons of God to incarnate in them, it was expedient that these incarnating minds should divide into halves, each half taking a body in conformity with its desires; in order that the new evolutionary scheme should be carried out in a shorter time than in former Cosmic Days.

When the war of minds was ended and each subjective mind or soul had become accustomed to the new order of things, it was delighted with its conditions. It found the earth a garden filled with flowers and trees, with which its taste for the beautiful could be gratified. There were also delicious fruits with which its appetite could be pleased and satisfied. And there were silver and gold and precious stones with which its person and its abiding place could be adorned. Everything was here that could please the eye and gratify the senses, and then to each mind came the desire for individual possessions and great accumulation of material things.

Then man's original vibrations began to grow more and more gross until the beautiful subjective blue and yellow which had characterized his innocence deepened into the darkest shade of a selfish myrtle green. The animal nature which he had espoused and had come to rule, rose in its desires and ruled him. He became enveloped in the dark red vibrations of its animal passions, and the combination of the selfish green vibrations with the sexual red drew him into the lowest depths of those two currents.[1] He sank lower than the animals because he had enough of the Divine Principle within him to give him reasoning power, by means of which he could better accomplish his purposes than could the animals.

This was "The Fall of Man," "The Original Sin," "The Fall from Grace," etc. But Divine Principle

---

[1]The History and Power of Mind, pp. 135-136; 228-230.

never goes backward. It is constantly pushing onward and upward; and although sometimes, from a
narrow point of view, it seems that men and things
are degenerating and retrograding beyond all hope
of recovery, still it is only seeming and not real.

When the subjective man plunged from his realm
of innocence and inexperience into the experiences of
this earth, he was negatively good. He had never
been tempted and had never come into contact with
anything of a lower rate of vibration than his own.
He was pure because his environment had been pure.
He was an infant mind or soul entering in upon a
new state of existence.

Because he had not experienced it, he did not know
that indulgence in sexual excesses would ruin his
body. Neither did he know that his generative organs had been made for the purpose of creating new
human bodies for other egos to incarnate in.

As it has always been with every race at every
great period of time since man came to live upon this
planet, the first egos who came to incarnate were
the stronger ones, possessing more persistence and
endurance than did those who arrived later. This
was a necessity in order that each new race should
have its pioneers, its strong men, to do the heavy
work and to prepare the way for the weaker ones
who would follow after them. When these pioneers
were struggling to overcome the wild beasts of the
forests and jungles and to prepare places in which
to live, their forces went into physical labor, and

they had neither time nor inclination to yield themselves to sexual excesses, to the same extent as did those who followed them. But as time passed the weaker egos incarnated in greater numbers. And when they could enjoy more comforts and luxuries than their progenitors, without the same efforts to obtain them, the morals of the peoples became more and more corrupt; and men and women began making the fearful mistake of thinking that their generative organs were created for the sole purpose of gratifying their own sexual, animal desires, and for the amusement and entertainment of their friends. They indulged themselves in every sexual excess that the human mind could devise until the time came to pay the penalty for attempting to break the Law of Being. Then men's magnificent physical strength began to leave them; they grew weak and ill and commenced to suffer the pains and aches and diseases which must necessarily follow upon those acts which drain the system of its precious, vital creative fluids.

Then the physical bodies of the offspring began to manifest weaknesses inherited from their parents. "There were giants in the earth in those days," but gradually the physical stature of the races grew less and the "Samsons" were fewer and farther apart, until in the course of a great number of re-incarnations or generations the man who originally, in the beginning of his race, had stood ten or twelve feet in height became reduced in stature to six or

eight feet and his physical strength decreased in pro-
portion.

But Divine Law has never left Its children without object lessons constantly before their eyes, and
had they been wise enough to take cognizance of
those lessons and had they profited by them much
suffering for the world would have been avoided.
Around men on every side was operating the law of
attraction and repulsion; they saw its effects, but
did not look for the causes. In their experience with
the mineral kingdom they learned how to combine
such minerals as were magnetically attracted toward
each other and became quite skillful in making for
themselves ornaments composed of such amalgama-
tions as they desired and admired. They knew that
the sex principle—which is but a higher expression
of the law of attraction and repulsion—manifested in
all organized life; and they also knew that there
were few sexual excesses or abuses committed among
the creatures of a lower grade of intelligence than
themselves. Yet still they remained willfully blind
to this great truth which Divine Law was gradually
trying to force upon them through suffering: that
the relation of sex in the human family should not
be a promiscuous relation, and that the generative
organs of man could not be prostituted without dire
results to the prostitutor.

According to the Divine Law, the union of the
sexes should never take place without the desire of
both the male and the female who participate in that

union; and the desire should never be stimulated by anything except the mutual magnetic attraction of each toward the other. Pictures which stimulate the passions, wines, liquors, drugs or highly spiced foods which befog the brain or produce unnatural and inordinate desires, should be abolished from civilized life, because the progressing man and woman cannot afford to have their development retarded by the use of them.

During the perfect sex union of normal human bodies there is an exchange of magnetic force which is strengthening both to the physical bodies and to the minds of each. This exchange of magnetic force is due to the fact that the generative organs of the male and female act upon each other as do the opposite poles of an electrical instrument. A perfect circuit is made between the two bodies, and at the point of direct contact heat, power and life are generated. Then the nerves and blood absorb this electric fluid which flows from one body to the other and they become electrified and strengthened; and with an electrified and strengthened body the mind gains power.

The primary use, however, of the union of sex is for the production of physical bodies for other egos to incarnate in. It is a sacred privilege to become the father or mother of another divine soul's earthly vehicle, and the generative organs of men and women should be kept sacred to the uses for which the Great Consciousness intended them.[1] Abuse of these or-

[1] The History and Power of Mind, pp. 89-90.

gans leads to the degradation of the abuser because it is consciously or unconsciously a blasphemous act against the highest and most sacred law of Divine Principle. For the perpetration of this crime man will continue to be punished so long as he continues to transgress, and the punishment will be of his own creation and he always precipitates it upon himself.

Prostitution of the generative organs of mankind is the most far-reaching and the most stupendous of all the mistakes he makes. It is the most difficult of all to correct because of the subtle influences which surround him. The false teachings of past ages must be met and overcome; his social environment affects him adversely, as does also his belief that the forgiveness of sins will remove the consequences of his acts. Then, too, connubial influences are often brought to bear upon him which he believes he cannot ignore. But the time has come when the law must be recognized and obeyed, and a further discussion of it will be given in the lectures entitled "Marriage" and "Parenthood."

There came a time with every race when it was almost impossible to find positive virtue in either sex. If a pure ego came to dwell among those people it received persecution, abuse and even crucifixion, for attempting to live on a higher plane of morality than that of its time. And when the races became so corrupt that they constantly despised purity and loved impurity, there was nothing that Divine Law could do to help their condition but to permit a cataclysm or a holocaust to sweep them off the earth, in order to begin a new period of evolution.

When we stand among the ruins of old Nineveh and trace the broken outlines of her immense proportions and realize that it was only about four thousand years ago that she was in the height of her glory, conquering and enslaving every other nation and tribe of men who dared exist within her mighty reach, we wonder what could have brought that great city, and the powerful nation of which she was the capital, to this condition of ruin and almost utter oblivion. For it is only by studying the now nearly obliterated inscriptions left upon her broken pillars and by piecing together her shattered tablets that the present race of men is able to learn anything about her. Among the remains of her once beautiful palaces and walls there are still to be found indications of the great skill of her workmen; and since all this is but the materialized expression of the mental force of that nation, we must acknowledge that in power of concentration and creation they were equal, if not superior, to many men of our present day.

Where is there to be found anything that our present race has created which required the time, the effort and the patience to build as did the great wall surrounding Nineveh? It stood, a solid piece of masonry, fifty feet in thickness, one hundred and fifty feet in height, and eight miles in length, and was at once a roof garden and a speedway, enclosing an area of one thousand and eight hundred acres of land com-

prising the city. It was built to give pleasure to
kings and princes, who, while testing the speed of
their horses upon it, enjoyed a fine view of the surrounding country; and it also made the city unap-
proachable and for a long time invincible to its enemies who wished to destroy it.

Within that great enclosure were palaces of such
immense proportions that the buildings of the present day in many respects seem almost insignificant
when compared with them. Not in height, perhaps,
did those great piles of stone exceed our own, but in
depth, breadth and thickness. Their massive pillars
and stairways, their entrances, their corridors and
their audience rooms were built upon a vastly larger
scale than anything the peoples of the present day
have yet attempted.

But those marble halls where dwelt the kings and
princes of that remote past are now nothing but huge
ash heaps. The magnificent apartments where the
noble lords and ladies of those days were born, grew
to manhood and womanhood, danced, sang, told tales
of love, wooed, wedded and died, are now reduced to
dust and debris. Not a living thing may be seen in
all that place of desolation except, perhaps, after
nightfall, from some crevice or pit the gleaming eyes
of a wild beast may peer out at the belated traveler;
and after the sun goes down nothing may be heard to
break the awful stillness except the growl of a savage
brute or the call of a night-bird.

All the mighty men of valor who once lived in that

now ruined city are gone, and not a descendant is left to-day to tell the tale of his forefathers' strength and prowess. But there are legends to be found concerning those Ninevite heroes, and through these we learn that their kings were warlike and their conquering soldiery made the earth tremble with their tremendous power. The same ferocity which they manifested in the pursuit and destruction of wild beasts they also exhibited in hunting their fellow men; and the dead of their vanquished foes they contemptuously trampled in the dust under their horses' feet.

But when these great wars were ended, because the surrounding nations and tribes which were accessible had been conquered and enslaved, the Ninevite kings and princes became weary of war and began yielding to the sensuousness and sensuality which comes to all wealthy and prosperous nations. They commenced feasting and dancing, wearing rich garments and fine jewels, and indulging in great sexual excesses. The later generations being composed of weaker egos, readily and willingly adopted the habits of their ancestors, and the progress of the nation paused, hesitated for a while, and then began to decline.

Indolence is the father of voluptuousness, and when those ancient men commenced to yield to the seductive influence of indolence, their tremendous forces sought expression through their lusts. They plunged into sexual indulgences and excesses with the same energy that they had fought battles and built palaces, and soon the Assyrian nation reached a point where there seemed to be no limit to its voluptuousness. The wives and daughters, the matrons, maids and slaves were not able to satisfy the lasciviousness of the men, and when the whole nation had become so corrupt that there was no purity to be found in the land, a good man came to one of the great gates of Nineveh and commenced to cry against the sin that was being committed there.

In the legend of our Bible this man was a prophet and he was called Jonah, which means "a dove." He was a human instrument, a messenger sent to that immoral city to bring the word of warning which Divine Mind sent to Its children before permitting their punishment to come upon them. This good man came to Nineveh eight hundred and sixty years before the Nazarine was born, and when he entered the city he cried aloud to the people whom he met upon the streets and said:

"Yet forty days and Nineveh shall be overthrown!"

To this startling prophecy the people of the threatened city began to listen, and when the king heard it he "arose from the throne," and, laying aside his royal robes, he "covered himself with sackcloth and ashes," and sent forth his proclamation throughout the city that men and beasts should be covered with sackcloth; and that all men should "cry mightily unto God," and that they should "turn every one from his evil way."

Because of this penitence and temporary reformation the cloud of destruction which had been slowly gathering over the doomed city was lifted and the sentence of immediate destruction was commuted. Unknown to the people a reprieve of forty years instead of forty days was granted them, during which time the nation had ample time to permanently reform and save itself from downfall.[1]

But like all unwise peoples who had preceded, and like many who have succeeded them, they soon grew weary of well doing. Constant prayer and fasting became monotonous and tiresome, and when the "forty days" had past and there were no visible signs of the promised destruction of their city the Ninevites gradually fell back into their old immoral ways of living- and Jonah and his prophecy were discredited.

When the forty years of respite had passed the Great Consciousness sent another good man to warn the Assyrian nation of its danger, but since the first prophecy had not been fulfilled the people did not believe in the second, and the last days of Assyria's greatness drew to an end. Then everything seemed to conspire with fate to overthrow the city of Nineveh, and when the tramp of the Midian soldiers was heard in the streets, the people—many of whom had never before seen a foreign foe, except in the position of a trembling captive—were seized with a great fear and fled in terror from the approaching host. Even the king, Saracus, took refuge in his palace and ordered his slaves to heap his goods into a funeral pyre for himself and for his household; and when the torch

---

[1] Mata the Magician, pp. 150-151; Cosmogony and Evolution, pp. 115-116.

was applied he covered his face with his mantle and his ashes were mingled with the ashes of the great city, where his ancesters had ruled and reigned for many generations before him. Nineveh was shrouded in everlasting night, destroyed by her blasphemous acts against the Divine Consciousness of which she was a part.

With the downfall of Nineveh the Babylonian Empire immediately sprang into prominence, and very soon became the supreme power of the Eastern World. The men were strong and hardy, with large physique, and became the most distinguished merchants of the age, as their nation continued to prosper in material wealth. Babylon became the great metropolis of Western Asia and the peoples of the old world turned to it for their supplies. Whatever mankind had to sell was offered in her markets, and whatever the world demanded was to be found there. In the beginning of the nation's career there was much to admire and very little to condemn, but as it grew richer and more prosperous and as the weaker egos of the older races came to re-incarnate in the Babylonian race, avarice and greed for wealth overcame all the higher principles of the people and the time came when the domestic virtues were recklessly flung away for further gratification. It became a law that every Babylonian woman once in her life must offer herself to strangers publicly before the temple of Beltis in order to attract to the city of Babylon the trade of strangers.

Maidens were sold at auction to wealthy princes and libertines who were thus induced to come to the city to spend their money. Both sexes were ready at any moment to barter for money the pleasures which should be sacred to love, and the prime motive for all this was the passion for luxurious living.

Babylon became the earthly paradise for gluttony and lust and whatever ministered to the appetites, and sensuality was eagerly enjoyed without scruple by the people. Rich garments and jewels of untold value were persistently sought for; and luxurious baths and fragrant oils for perfuming the body, costly viands and rare foods were provided for those who could afford to pay for them. Everything that could excite or appease human desire was demanded, found and wasted in luxurious abandonment. The banquet and feast brought drunkenness and revel. The tables were spread with food of such richness that no human being could consume it. Dark wines were drunk from goblets of gold; delicious fruits were piled high upon platters of silver. Palaces became harems and polygamy the custom of the whole nation.

In spite of all their love of luxury the men were fearless soldiers, and it is said that their courage in war was equal to their abandonment to pleasure. They were nearly always at war with surrounding nations, and from the mountains to the gates of Egypt their merciless, lascivious soldiery carried the banners of their Empire before which all other nations cringed. As a natural consequence their successes made them a haughty and an austere people. Pride came with their power as avarice had grown with their gain, and lust from their lawless indulgences. Babylon sat as a queen of the East, and her royal broods of princes and pampered idlers found nothing to check their selfishness and their vanity.

But notwithstanding all these things, in no country, except in Egypt, were the ceremonies of religion more carefully observed. Temples arose on every side. Priests, engaged in the work peculiar to their supposedly sacred offices, were always to be seen. The dissolute kings were chief worshippers at the holy shrines and princes went devoutly to the temples. The seals and charms worn by both sexes were embellished with some religious device or emblem, and when the feasts were spread and the banqueters became uproariously drunk over their wines they invariably sang songs in honor of their gods.

At all times these people cultivated a placid external manner and prided themselves upon their ability to commit the worst outrages with smiling faces. The city was laid out in blocks or squares, their buildings were three or four stories in height, and altogether in many respects New York, Chicago and San Francisco of to-day are not dissimilar to Babylon in architecture or in mode of living.

It is not at all difficult to trace in our "kings of finance," our "political bosses," our "rings" and "machines" the same characters who debauched the nation and themselves in Babylon. In many of our shop

women, who are expected to entertain traveling sales-
men and merchants who go to a city to buy goods and
otherwise to spend their money, we are able to discern
the same characters who offered themselves to
strangers before the temple of Beltis. And the men
and women of fashion who pass their precious time in
gaming and who have no regard for the sacredness of
their marriage vows gained their proficiency in such
matters as far back as the Babylonian times. And since
so many persons are lacking in a knowledge of the
great truth that a pure relationship between the sexes
must be established on earth before our race can reach
a higher point of development and before real happiness can be gained, it looks as though the people of the
present age would have to meet the same fate as those
of the past in order that they should learn the lesson
which God—the Great Consciousness—is trying to
teach.

During the early part of the life of Nebuchadnezzar
the Babylonian nation reached its zenith of wealth
and power, and at that time the vices of the people
were greatest. The king himself set the example of
cruelty and selfishness to his people, who were delighted to follow his leading. Murder and rapine
were his chief amusements, and the suffering of his
victims seemed to give him the greatest pleasure. But
when well advanced in age this monarch dreamed the
prophetic dream which foretold his approaching
downfall, and from that day his power and the power
of the nation began to wane.

When Belshazzar came to the throne the downfall of the nation was close at hand. But in his contempt for an enemy whom he believed to be powerless to harm him, he recklessly gave himself to the enjoyment of a great annual festival of the Babylonians. A thousand nobles were present at the banquet. There was splendor within the palace and darkness without, and while the drunken revel was at its height the enemy stole like a thief in the night and opened the river sluices into the canals and the river began to sink. Then there was nothing to prevent the foe from entering the gates and the city was at its mercy. The drunken Babylonians then received the kind of treatment that they had given to others in the past. Their karma had fallen upon them, and the prophecy of Isaiah was fulfilled:

"And Babylon, the glory of kingdoms, the beauty of Chaldees' excellency shall be as when God overthrew Sodom and Gomorrah. It shall never be inhabited, neither shall it be dwelt in from generation to generation, neither shall the Arabian pitch his tent there; neither shall the shepherds make their folds there. But the wild beasts of the desert shall lie there and their houses shall be full of doleful creatures; and owls shall dwell there and satyrs shall dance there."

And the condition of Babylon to-day is the same that it was after its destruction over two thousand years ago.

The ancient Romans were an improvement upon the Babylonians because of the experiences the egos had received in Babylon previous to their incarnating in Rome. Monogamy was the law in the beginning of the Roman period, and motherhood was respected and domestic ties were recognized, and Roman fathers had a parental feeling for their children. They recognized their sons as their rightful heirs and their daughters as the prospective matrons of Rome.

In early times the Roman table was spread in the plainest manner and the fare was Spartan-like in its simplicity; but about one hundred and seventy years before the Nazarene was born they began to import and enjoy the gastronomic luxuries of the East. With feasting came drinking, and these indulgences continued and increased until in a few years the life of the wealthy Romans became bestial to a degree never before equalled by civilized people.

As the people of Rome gained in wealth they commenced spending it in riotous living, and finally the time came when the whole city was a scene of revelry and dissipation. To show the slow development which has been made by the incarnating souls of to-day, we may compare the Roman amusements and customs with those of our own age. The disregard of the duties and responsibilities of life and the love of amusement led the Roman people to accept as their motto and demand, "Bread and the circus," and Rome was as well supplied with circuses as New York is supplied with theatres. It was "bread and the circus" then for all the people; it is now bread and the theatre for some of the people.

When the circus became tame and uninteresting and the people desired that blood should be spilled for their amusement, the Gladiators' time arrived. When some of the people of this age desired that blood should be drawn for their amusement the prize ring was inaugurated, and the reincarnated gladiators reappeared as contestants.

When the Romans went into battle they beheaded or enslaved their prisoners. When the men of our time go into battle they kill as many of the enemy as they can and collect indemnity to pay for their wasted ammunition, and so evolution goes on.

We who are living in the twentieth century are the Ninevites, the Babylonians and the Romans. Are we to be swept out of this life in the same inglorious manner as at those other periods of our existence? Shall we go out from this incarnation in disgrace and humiliation because of our failure to learn that the right relation of the sexes is the rock foundation for all mankind to build the house of life upon, and because we fail to read the writing upon the walls of our individual palaces? Or, shall we turn from our follies and vices and save ourselves and our children from a repetition of those mistakes?

True it is that each individual must ultimately stand or fall for itself; but it is also true that each ego has its influence to help or to hinder others upon their evolutionary journey. And the higher one stands socially, politically or financially, the more harm one does or the more help one gives to others; for it is by example that one really teaches.

Can we say to our children "be pure," "be truthful," "be honest," when we ourselves are impure, untruthful or dishonest? Can men and women who stand at the head of a nation expect or hope that the lesser social or political lights of that nation, which they represent, will shine brighter than they?

Our Shalmanesers, our Sargons, our Nebuchadnezzars, our Belshazzars and our Ptolemys, as well as our Cæsars, our Neros, and our Napoleons are all here. And we also have our Semiramis, our Amyitis, our Cleopatra and our Josephine among us to-day. The same force which each of those individual egos manifested as ancient characters is still theirs and is manifesting now.

It may be that the Cæsars and Napoleons of to-day are rulers of finance, or they may be the most unscrupulous politicians. Our Cleopatra and our Josephine may be women of fashion, shop girls or housemaids; but they are here and are playing their parts upon the stage in this drama of life. And while we are studying the subject "From Incarnation to Reincarnation" let each individual begin by asking itself these questions:

"What am I doing in this twentieth century? Am I progressing or retrogressing? If I am Cæsar, am I doing better or worse than I did in Rome? If I am Cleopatra, have I learned anything by my past experiences or am I making the same mistakes over and over again that I made in Egypt?"

LECTURE TWO.

MARRIAGE.

Before man divided and incarnated in the animal forms of earth, he was negatively good and blissfully happy, with that happiness which comes with inertness and passivity. He needed nothing, which he did not have, that was necessary for his condition at that time, because he was a part of Divine Consciousness, and his existence was forever established. As the tree draws life from the surrounding atmosphere and from the earth in which it is implanted, so did the Sons of God live on the Universal Consciousness which surrounded them. Development and growth were impossible under those contented and blissful conditions; and had not that Eden garden been abolished, evolution on that plane would have come to a standstill.

Those Sons of God could be of no assistance to each other, because all things were equally distributed, and there was no opportunity to be either selfish or generous. There was nothing for them to do, because all had been done that could be done in that realm, and there was "nothing to live but life." Under those conditions stagnation was inevitable, but nowhere in all the universe is absolute stagnation permitted to exist. Throughout all parts of Deity, during each Cosmic Day there must be activity. And so Divine Mind sent Its Sons to this earth to find what was not to be found on their Eden planet.

Ever since those Sons of God incarnated on earth, each half has been earnestly seeking a re-union with the other part of itself. Sub-consciously each one holds a mental picture of his past happiness, when, in the realm of innocence and purity, he dwelt free from the ills and troubles of his present state of existence. And each one longs for a return to the old blissful condition, for happiness is what every human soul desires more than anything else in the world, and it is for happiness that every one is striving.

With Divine Man's descent into this material realm he forgot his origin, and the further he wandered among the forests and in the fields of sense the deeper he drank of the waters of Lethe. But in an inner chamber of each heart, where none can enter or disturb, there is a picture of another face which looks smilingly out and seems to beckon to the seeker after happiness, and says: "I am the one that you desire. When you find and possess me you will have your wish, for I am happiness."

Perhaps Man does not know it, but this picture is of the other half of himself, the only one in all the Universe whose basic vibrations correspond with his own. He loves it, but he knows not why. And should he be an artist he tries to reproduce it upon his canvas. If he is a musician he composes and sings to it.

If an actor he plays his best when he thinks he sees it among his audience. If he is a man of finance he saves money for it, and dreams of the day when, in human form, it will sit at his table, wear his jewels and be his life-long companion. Sometimes he has a fancy that he has seen it. A woman whom he meets reminds him of his sacred picture. There is a look or a gesture which he believes he remembers, and eagerly he seeks an introduction. It may or may not be the one he is looking for; if it is and a marriage is consummated between them, his longing is satisfied. There will be no other face so dear and no other form so precious as hers. If he is a man well on in his development, he will always be true to her, and should she be taken from him by the transition called death, he would never seek to fill, with another, the place in his heart that she occupied. Should he be an undeveloped man with animal passions unrestrained, he would, in his brutal way, always love her best, but she might not be his only love.

When an ego seeking happiness incarnates in female form, the precious picture of the other half of herself still remains in the sacred inner chamber of her heart. It is the same dear face that she has always loved and has been seeking through all the lives that she has lived. But now, perhaps, her fancy paints it dressed in military garments, or perhaps it may be that he wears the royal ermine and a crown. And if not either one of these, perhaps she sees him in other walks of life, among the professions or in the trades. For in the midst of what a woman most admires, there she puts her sacred picture and there she does her worshipping.

If the law of compensation has decreed that a woman shall not meet her other half in a lifetime, she may enter into what the world calls a marriage of convenience. In this case, if her moral principles are well established, she is faithful to the man she has espoused, and makes what the world calls a good wife; but in the sanctuary of her soul is the image of her true love, her real husband; and when she is tried with the cares and vexations of her wedded life, and her heart aches with its emptiness, she turns to her sacred picture and for the time being is comforted.

Marriage is the re-union of the two halves of an ego, and any other union which in any way imitates it, is necessarily a mock-marriage. When two mismated halves attempt to consummate a union, it is but an abortive attempt at marriage, and is never perfectly satisfactorily to either. When we stop to consider how many millions of half souls are dwelling upon this globe to-day, and when we realize that there are at least half as many more on the subjective planes surrounding the earth, and that from among this vast multitude there are only two whose basic vibrations are the same, and who belong to each other, it is not difficult to understand why mock-marriages are so numerous. That they are a necessity to a certain point, during the evolutionary work that has to be done, no one can deny. At this time they are helpful to those who engage in them, because they bring experiences which are necessary in order that marriage may be understood and appreciated. There is no contract which a man makes that is so far reaching in its ramifications as the legalized marriage contract. It effects, for good or ill, more persons than does any other contract; and it not only colors the life in which it is made, but it sometimes influences following incarnations.

No ego knows what it is capable of doing or of becoming until it has been tried. It must indeed be ground upon the wheel of fine experiences before the brilliancy of its mind jewels can shine forth; and the mock-marriage covenant provides for it the greatest wheel in the machinery of life, while Divine Law turns it slowly or rapidly, as the exigencies of the case require.

The question is often asked: "Is marriage a failure?" and the disgruntled victims of mock-marriages sometimes spend weeks and months in writing articles devoted to this great subject. They believe they are doing the world and their fellowmen a service by holding their personal miseries up to view, and they seem to get satisfaction from telling the world about the troubles wedded life has brought to them. They do not know that during all the lives that they have lived upon this planet, they have, perhaps, never been really married one dozen times, and often even those few experiences of connubial bliss are entirely forgotten.

But, like all other false things, mock-marriage must some time be destroyed. When its purpose has been served in the evolutionary scheme it will disappear from the face of the earth, and marriage, for which mock-marriage is but a poor substitute, will take its place.

It is a comfort, perhaps, to know that as the human race evolves, half souls meet oftener and enjoy the privilege of each other's society for longer periods of time. And as these unions are made more often, a deeper consciousness comes with each and the evolution of egos is thereby hastened.

It is a well known fact that the time for boy and girl weddings is practically ended, in the Western world at least; brides of sixteen and bridegrooms of twenty are now the exception and not the rule, as they once were. It is no longer a disgrace for a woman to go through life alone if she feels so disposed. There are no more "old maids," and if there were there is not sufficient opprobrium attached to the title to frighten girls into making mock-marriages to escape it. The woman who prefers not to wed but to remain true to her ideal—the sacred picture which she carries in her heart—is evincing a courage which many of her weaker married sisters would do well to emulate.

And the "old bachelor," who is attacked on every side by matrons, maids and unhappy benedicts, because, for a given reason or without one, he refuses to be inveigled into a distasteful mock-marriage for the sake of some one else's convenience, is really a pioneer—although perhaps he does not know it—in the ranks of those who will in the future be instrumental in abolishing mock-marriages. Because he does not wed there is no reason to suppose that he has not his sacred picture in his heart, and that he does not worship at that shrine the same as do all other half souls.

As evolution goes on and egos increase in strength and positive goodness, the Law of Attraction, acting along the line of least resistance, will bring half souls together even without the aid of their own conscious, mental demands, while mismated egos will be, by the law of repulsion, separated and swept apart more quickly than before.

Many kindly disposed persons are regretting the fact that the "divorce mills are grinding by night and by day," and are separating husbands and wives by the hundreds and thousands. The anxiety of these good people might be quieted, perhaps, by the knowledge that it is not an evil, but a good, that they are so earnestly deploring. The divorce mills never separate the husbands and wives who truly belong to each other, but only those mismated persons who have entered into mock-marriages which they can no longer endure.

While recognizing the unhappiness of many mock-marriages, yet it is shocking to the man or woman who understands the holy relationship of marriage to listen to the ridicule and contemptuous remarks that are constantly being made about it in many of our theatres and at other places of amusement. The supposedly funny men use this sacred subject for an object at which to fire their witticisms. They rack their brains trying to study out some new sarcasm concerning it; and as fast as they fling their sacrilegious jokes at the public, the daily and weekly papers report and illustrate them with cartoons and caricatures to make them the more convincing and impressive.

It is true that the jokes nearly always bring a laugh from the mismated egos who are or have been suffering from the inconveniences or miseries of a mock-marriage, but a laugh is not always an expression of pleasure; sometimes it is but a thin veil for a sob, and very often those who laugh do so because they do not know what else to do.

Just a step below the loveless mock-marriage is another unhappy condition to which men and women often turn in desperation, hoping at least to escape from the limitations and bondage which the mock-marriage covenant so often puts upon its victims. This condition is prostitution of the sacred, generative organs, and is but another escape valve for the surging emotions and passions of those who are seeking but have not found the other half of themselves. Thousands of misguided people are wallowing in this slough of despond called prostitution. It is a dismal, dirty place to be in and he who enters it is not happy and never can be so long as he stays there.

Prostitution is called by various names according

to the grade or depth to which a person has sunk in it; for there are degrees in this as well as in all other kinds of experiences which man encounters on this plane of existence. In its beginning prostitution is never called by its rightful name; if it were, now that the human race has reached its majority, or age of understanding, it is probable that many egos would hesitate and perhaps be spared much suffering which comes through indulgence in this vice. But society and the world at large use a softer, gentler word to designate this crime, and as a consequence the tempted ones are lulled into a false sense of security by the use of the wrong title.

It does not shock the sensitiveness of a woman who has just entered the by-path of unchastity to say, "she has a love affair," "a little aside," or "a private romance." But if she were to be told instead that she had become a prostitute, and had started for hell, she might pause and consider, and perhaps turn away from the temptation altogether.

At its beginning the road of prostitution often assumes the appearance of a beautiful, restful pathway hedged by sweetest flowers and entered through a love bower of roses. A tempter in human form always stands at the entrance to this bower and smilingly invites all passers-by to enter and enjoy the seductive influences to be found within. If it is a heartbroken woman who is passing, the tempter knows that she is wedded to a humanized brute, and it assumes the appearance of a thoughtful, kindly man. Perhaps he may come to her in the form of her physician, her attorney, her priest or her pastor. At first he looks the sympathy he dares not express to her in words, and she feels rested and comforted in his presence. After a while he tells her to come inside the bower which stands at the entrance to the by-path, and rest a while with him, and she, craving the love of which she has been defrauded in her wedded life, steps aside, believing she will find within that bower what her heart longs for.

If the passer-by is a disappointed man wedded to a woman who has no sympathy with him; if he is aspiring to heights of fame or fortune which seem unattainable, unaided and alone, the tempter at the entrance to the bower appears to him in the form of a woman, an intellectual and social leader of society, perhaps. She tells him he is worthy of a better place than the one he occupies, and that he can never rise to the heights he wishes to gain so long as he is held in bondage to the "clod" that he has wedded. She flatters and offers to help him gain the position he so much desires, and he steps inside the love bower, believing it to be the entrance to a higher life.

If the passer-by is a poor girl, earning her bread and the bread for some one dependent upon her, the tempter appears to her in the form of a man possessed of an abundance of the world's goods. He tells her that she is fitted for a better life than the one she is living; that with her beauty and her grace she should be gowned in silks and satins, and that jewels should shine from among the locks of her beautiful hair and sparkle against her soft, velvety skin. He whispers love into her ears and promises to share his wealth with her if she will but step into the love bower with him. If she listens and accepts his invitation, she, too, has started for the slough of despond called prostitution.

If it is a young man just starting in life with his physical body filled with strength and animal magnetism, the tempter appears to him in the form of a handsome, dashing, laughing woman. She promises to give him excitement that will make the nerves of his body throb with delight. She offers amusements and pleasures most exquisite if he will enter the love bower with her; and when he has entered she points out the road beyond which she says leads to a long life and a happy one. She is mistaken. She is pointing the way to a short life and a wretched one; to nothing but the fleeting pleasures of sensuality.[1] For pleasure is not happiness. It is created only by the temporary gratification of the physical senses, and may be turned into pain in an instant of time, while happiness is harmony and may last so long as the ego exists. It may be enjoyed in the humblest as well as the most exalted positions in which man may live upon this earth. It is the light which shines from within outward, and it is not dependent upon external things for its existence or intensity.

In man's progress and search for happiness on

---

[1] Mata the Magician, pp. 123-125.

earth he seems to find it necessary to investigate and explore all the by-ways which lead from the highway of life. Just opposite to the by-way of prostitution is another one leading in an opposite direction. It is a much narrower path and more difficult to follow, and is called celibacy. It is never found nor tried by any one until after that one has lived through a few lives of prostitution, with their attending miseries. Then, with soul filled with loathing or with fear of the consequences of sexual indulgences and excesses, the ordinary celibate rushes to the opposite extreme and enters into a life of sexual repression.

If he becomes fanatical upon the subject, he shuts himself away from the world and refuses to see or speak to a woman. Perhaps he finds a few others who are smarting under similar afflictions, and he prevails upon them to join him in forming a society or brotherhood, which they agree to call a holy order, and perhaps the remainder of that life will be spent where they cannot be reached by their former temptations. In their desire to live apart from the world they sometimes retire to the mountains and build such barriers between them and their fellow-men as will guard them from what they believe to be their greatest enemy—women—and there they undertake to do God's will.

Since all kinds of experiences are necessary to the development of an ego, this kind of life, from an evolutionary standpoint, is a sort of resting place where man stops in his career while he reviews his past experíences and assimilates the good that is to be gained from them. The life of the celibate is a long step in advance of the life of prostitution, and there can be no doubt that in this new position man gains an advantage over the other kind of life. But if he has become a celibate because of his hatred for women, or because he fears that he is not strong enough to meet and overcome the temptations that the world holds for him, then he has not conquered his passions, and the Divine Law will force him back into the world in some future life to finish fighting the battles from which he has fled.

Fear brings limitation of thought, and a limitation of thought brings a limitation of freedom. It is the fear of persons or of things which causes a man or a woman to live voluntarily behind iron-bound doors and within solid walls of masonry. And the great piles of stone into which they retire for protection from the world, the flesh and the devil are but stupendous monuments to their fears. The power and extent of a celibate's fear are usually represented by the size of the monument he builds for himself, and although he may retire within it and live for a lifetime, he has not escaped from Divine Law, which will bring to him in another life everything that he feared and ran from in this one.[1]

If a man becomes a celibate because he is afraid of the consequences of living a life of prostitution, and if his desires for sex union are strong within him,

[1]The History and Power of Mind, pp. 84-90.

then the continued and enforced repression of the physical expression of those desires will produce a congested condition of his generative organs, and also of all other organs which are sympathetically connected with them. He has not escaped from the consequences of his desires for sexual union, nor from the result of the physical repression of those desires.

Many physicians declare that celibacy produces monomaniacs, fools and lunatics, and advise their patients to indulge, rather than repress, their sexual desires, calling such indulgences "physical necessities." The Occultist says that the true principle of celibacy is represented by the person who lives the life of chastity because he loves chastity, and not because he fears consequences or future punishment. And when that point has been reached in his evolution, he has no fear of persons or of things tempting him to stray from the path of purity; and he will not become a lunatic nor a fool, nor will his life be spent within the walls of a monastery.

The Century Dictionary defines chastity as, The state or quality of being chaste; the state of being guiltless of unlawful sexual intercourse; sexual purity; celibacy; the unmarried state; abstinence from lawful indulgences in sexual intercourse; continence due to a religious motive.

There was once a man who said that virtue or chastity was like an onion. It had many layers or skins, and the deeper one went toward the heart of it, the thicker the skins became. The Century Dictionary's definition of chastity gives the word as many shades of meaning as there are skins to an onion; and after reading the various definitions, it is really left to the one seeking the truth to decide to which shade or layer he belongs or aspires.

To the man sodden in debaucheries, the person who indulges in an occasional "aside," or "romance," represents his ideal of chastity; and to the man with an occasional "affair," the one who does not violate the letter of his marriage vows is a chaste person. Physical virtue is what most persons call chastity, and the world thinks it matters not what impure things may be thought or said by either a man or a woman, if neither actually break the seventh commandment.

This is not getting very deep into the onion, but it is a small gain and shows that the race has made some progress since the Ninevite and Babylonian times. But physical chastity alone is not to be trusted or depended upon. It is like any other negative goodness, and may be maintained so long as the environment conducive to that condition exists; or it may become corrupted at any moment when temptation is placed before it. To be of lasting value it must have the sustaining power of a pure mind behind it. And this condition is never reached in the career of any ego until it has gained a point in its development where it really desires to be chaste for chastity's sake, and not for the sake of individual or public opinion.

The world has the mistaken belief that the sweet privilege of chastity should be granted only to the feminine portion of humanity, and that it is exclusively a feminine requisite and most unbecoming to the sterner portion, the masculine element of society. To this great misconception of the truth is much of the domestic sorrow of to-day attributable, and the progress of the race must necessarily be retarded as long again as it would be if men recognized their own need of chastity. For so long as men continue to believe that because of the majesty of their sex they are divinely and socially licensed individuals, and that the seventh commandment, or any other rule or code of moral regulations, applicable to women, is not applicable to them or to their conduct in life, the human race will make very slow progress. Unless both sexes build their characters upon the rock foundation of chastity, their life structures cannot withstand the storms of experience which come to every incarnated ego.

How can one half of the population of the earth attain or maintain a condition of purity while the other half is working to overthrow and destroy that condition? Solomon, who was reputed to be the wisest man who had ever lived during ancient Bible times, asked: "Who can find a virtuous woman?" and then followed his question with the declaration: "For her price is far above rubies." If the Bible stories are true concerning his moral character, he was responsible for much of the scarcity of virtue among the women of his time; and when he complained of their impurity he was like the men who spend all their money in riotous living and then blame society and the government for their poverty. Solomon manifested a great lack of wisdom when he complained of a condition that he was using his kingly influence to produce; and Occultists would never enroll his name among the names of their wise men.

There are men who take great pride in declaring that they are honest. They point to long periods of commercial integrity and perhaps challenge their fellow-men to find one dishonest act in their career. Because they have not stolen money or worldly goods, or have never taken a dishonorable advantage of their fellows in commercial life, they actually believe they have a right to be considered honest.

A man is often heard to say: "I never break a promise. My word is as good as my bond," and while it may be true that he is scrupulously faithful to his commercial promises, at the same time he may be untruthful in his marriage relationship.

How can a man claim, or believe himself to be an honest or a just man when he ruthlessly breaks the most sacred promises he has made? If he takes a woman's hand and says to the world: I take this woman to be my wife and I will leave all others for her sake; I will cleave to her in sickness and in health, for better, for worse; I will love, protect and shield her from the world and be true to her until death parts us; his promise will influence for good or ill not only the incarnation in which it was made, but it may also influence many future incarnations.

And then if he steals away like a thief in the night and, while pretending to be what he is not, indulges his lower animal nature in sexual gratification with other women he is not an honest man.

When he returns to the wife who believes, trusts and perhaps loves him, and tells her falsehoods about his enforced absences, or if he acts the lies he does not speak, he is unjust and dishonorable and is unworthy of the respect of honest men and women.

The Occultist would say that to be honest a man must fulfill every promise—those made to women as well as those made to men; that honesty and truthfulness, like charity, must begin at home and extend outward into the social and financial circles in which men and women meet and mingle in the many affairs of life.

When the Sons of God forgot their origin and became enamoured of the pleasures of sense, they first adopted the system of communal marriage. This was largely due to the influence of the animal minds which they had espoused and against which they were unable to contend. In establishing a union of this kind a number of persons of both sexes who were comparatively congenial, agreed to become a community and to live apart from all other communities and to possess all things in common. This was the commencement of socialism. In a communal union of this kind the male percentage of offspring was irregular and uncertain. The mothers of the children became the absolute heads of the households, and the lineage of each individual could be traced only through its female ancestry. Since evolution can proceed only through individualization, and since communal unions were one of the grossest forms of prostitution, there could be but one result growing out of such relationship, and that was the destruction of those communities either by reason of a mutinous element arising within them, or by their being conquered and enslaved by a stronger tribe of men.

Out of the communal union there evolved two other systems of marital relationship, one called Polyandry and the other Polygamy, and each system was adopted according as it seemed best adapted to the climate and productiveness of the country in which the people lived. If some of the Sons of God migrated to a place where nature did not produce abundantly, and where they had to till the soil in order to live, or if they were driven by an enemy into the mountains where there were not opportunities for securing food through cultivating the soil, then large families were not desirable, and the marital system of Polyandry was adopted. By this system one woman became the wife of a family of brothers, the oldest brother making the selection of her, and the younger ones accepting his choice for the family wife without criticism or complaint. This was but a slight improvement upon the communal union, but it was an improvement, inasmuch as it limited the circle of possible parentage to a family rather than to a community.

But if man lived in a land where an abundance of food was to be had without effort, and if for shelter he needed only to interlace the boughs of a few saplings together and then permit the wild rose or grape vines to grow over them, making for him a comfortable abiding place, then he adopted the marital system of Polygamy for his sex union and raised large families of children. Under this system the lineage of each individual in a tribe was traceable through its male ancestry.

When humanity had reached a point where history began, in the Bible records, it was supposed to be the duty of every man to do his uttermost toward fulfilling the command in Genesis: "Be fruitful and multiply and replenish the earth and subdue it." It was then considered a disgrace to the head of a family not to be able to produce abundantly through his marital relationship. In those days a "barren woman" was a reproach to her sex, for she was believed to be under the curse of God, and her husband was justified by the customs of the times in "putting her away," while he brought another woman to fill her place in his home and to bear him children. Polygamy was freely practiced by men who thought it their duty—as well as pleasure—to use every available means toward swelling the size of the race to which they belonged. This order of things was continued, and by some nations recognized as a religious duty, until the ten commandments were given to Moses for the benefit of the Children of Israel. That

was the first religious check put upon polygamy, and
that was not very far reaching, since it only put a
limit upon man's sexual relations between himself
and other men's wives.   He was still permitted to
have as many wives as he could provide for if he confined his selections to unmarried women.   But nothing is ever to be gained for a nation through the practice of polygamy except numerical strength.   In every
other respect the practice is debasing and demoralizing.

As a nation or race advances in evolution the
Divine Law brings reforms; and in spite of the mixed
desires of the mass of humanity, a way will be found
to improve their condition.   There was never a tribe
or a nation so gross or so sensual that it did not have
its wise men who were stronger than those whom they
undertook to teach.   And those men who were in advance of the ignorant masses became the spiritual
advisers of not only the people, but also of the kings
and rulers.   Many of the wise men, the High Priests
of ancient Bible times, were Occultists and understood
that marriage meant the re-union of two souls; and
when those ancient peoples had evolved to a point
where they would listen to, and be influenced by, their
wise men on the subject of marriage, the High Priests
made the attempt to establish monogamy among
them.

When the priests were unable to determine whether
those who wished to marry really belonged to each
other or not, they consulted the stars, which were

supposed to indicate at the birth of each individual the exact point of development he had reached during his previous life. If the stars indicated adversely then the banns were forbidden, and the marriage was not consummated. But if they indicated favorably, the wedding was sanctified by a most solemn sacrament, and during the performance of the religious marriage rites the command was given forth by the officiating priest, "Whom God hath joined together let no man put asunder!"

It is to this fragment of Occult teachings that the Church of to-day holds as a reason for its refusal to recognize the union by contract or the modern divorce. And although it still attempts to enforce what it believes to be the command of God, and refuses to believe in human power to annul a marriage, still it does not take the trouble to first ascertain whether or not it is the sacred re-union of half souls which is being consummated, or even if there is a psychic or physical affinity between them. It bestows its blessing freely and indiscriminately upon all alike, and expects, notwithstanding the ignorance of the persons entering into a covenant of this kind, that it shall be maintained until the end of their natural lives. It is quite willing to forgive and absolve from consequences any mistake which man makes except his matrimonial mistakes; but these which are the most serious of all, and which affect more persons than any others, the Church does not permit him to correct.

The contractual union is the outgrowth of the natural consequences which followed many matrimonial mistakes and their attendant miseries. Smarting under what seemed to him an injustice inflicted by the Church in refusing to release him from his unhappy marital relationship, he conceived the plan of legalizing, by civil law, any contract which should appeal to his reason and sense of justice and which would protect his rights and those of his progeny.

This kind of union does not ask for itself the blessings of either priest or Church. The contract is usually prepared by an attorney and, like all other legal documents of any value, is signed, witnessed and recorded in the county or state where it was made. It is a cold-blooded, unromantic way of announcing to the world that a man and woman have agreed to enter into, what should be, the sacred relationship that exists between the true husband and wife; but because of the undevelopment of the mass of humanity, now incarnated upon earth, it seems to be a necessity at present. And since comparatively few marry for a reason other than for social or financial advantage, the contractual union serves its purpose very well indeed; and the victims of a mock-marriage seeking a legal separation or divorce are, by reason of this contract, saved the humiliation of receiving condemnation from the Church—since it cannot punish what it does not recognize.

If an American girls buys a duke for the sake of gaining a social position, it is because she is at a point in her development where she needs and deserves all the experiences which follow the making of such a purchase. If a nobleman barters his title for American dollars and accepts a girl as a necessity in the trade, he also needs, and will get, the experiences which will follow the making of his bargain, and there is no moral difference between this and any other trade. It is not a marriage, nor should it pretend to be. It is nothing but a union of the sexes as represented and expressed by those two individuals, and there is nothing more sacred about it than there is in hiring a mistress or buying a horse and cart.

It is not a violation of God's command to separate such persons by divorce, because God never joined them together; and it is to such business unions as these that the written contracts of marriage best fit. It gives to the offspring of such a union its legal property rights and a respectful recognition by the world, and it gives to the woman the privilege of using for the remainder of that life the particular crest and title belonging to the house in which she has bought a seat.

Among persons in other walks of life the same rule holds good. A loveless sex union is well evidenced by a written contract, and until the human race has evolved beyond its present condition and has reached a point where it understands and appreciates the sacredness of the esoteric basis of marriage, the Church union will in most cases be but a burlesque of the sacrament.

But the mock-marriage, with all its numerous disadvantages and unpleasant features, whether it be consummated through a contract or by the religious rites of a marriage sacrament, is a necessity at this time in the evolution of the race. Without its restraining influences upon the desires and passions of mankind, there would be no foundation for either positive or negative virtue to rest upon. Without it there would be nothing upon which to build our homes or our governments, and the human race would be no better off to-day than it was when might was right and every man was a free lance to do with his own and other's property as pleased him best. Mock-marriage is not only a social and political necessity, but it is a karmic necessity as well, and through it many egos are brought together in the family circle to work out past obligations and to pay debts which could be paid in no other way.

The Law of Justice does rule the world, although the contrary sometimes may appear to be true; and it operates in the most infinitesimal affairs and relations of life. If a man and a woman have entered into a mock-marriage there was a karmic reason for it; one or the other, or both, perhaps, owed a karmic debt which had to be paid; and it could be faithfully and fully done only through the devotion which is demanded and received through a covenant of this kind. If all persons who are chafing under the restraint caused by their matrimonial fetters would but realize that their present condition of unhappiness is but the result of past mistakes, of unjust treatment which they have given in some other life to the very individual they are now joined to in wedlock, it would serve to explain many of the mysteries and miseries of wedded life.

There is a way to become free from the unpleasant conditions which attend a mock-marriage, even though it has been karmically produced. It is through the power of mental demand. It is the divine right and privilege of every human being to demand of Divine Mind its freedom from unpleasant environment. And if this is done and the demand goes forth into the Great Consciousness with all the earnestness of a suffering soul, the fetters will begin to fall away, and one after another the limitations will be broken. The liberation will come in the way which Divine Mind wishes and which, in view of all past mistakes and injustices, is best for the one who makes the demand.[1] This subject will be again referred to in the lecture, "Mental and Spiritual Development."

Since it is through the marital relationship that a race continues to exist and evolve, it is most important that it should be brought to the highest point of refinement, and should be maintained in that position by the social and political power of the race.

With the picture of unhappy marital relationship constantly before the eyes of the people, there are many individuals of both sexes who are seeking relief from their dissatisfied or wretched conditions by en-

[1] The History and Power of Mind, pp. 150-162.

tering into what is called an "independent sex life."

The Church says: "Therefore (because woman was taken out of man) shall a man leave his father and his mother and shall cleave unto his wife, and they shall be one flesh." And the unhappy married man or woman says: "That may or may not be true, but if it is, why should I be made to suffer a deprivation of agreeable sex relationship with some one I like better than the person I am married to, because thousands of years ago a woman was taken out of a man?"

Then the State says to the would-be independent sex relationist: "I will punish you with fine or imprisonment if you commit adultery or fornication." And the seeker after sexual freedom replies: "Then I will hide the truth from you; I will do in secret what I am not permitted to do openly."

And then commence the falsehoods which this man or woman must tell in order to be protected from the penalties which follow the living of a double life. When an individual commences to lie about a particular thing, he often loses his scruples concerning all kinds of falsehood and sinks to the lowest degree of prevarication and deception. His word becomes of no value to his friends nor to society in general, and after a while he receives nothing but contempt from his fellow men. When he has ceased to tell the truth he has ceased to love it, and if he does not love the truth he will be untrue to himself and to every one else.

But this is not all that is to be dreaded by the un-

truthful man or woman. There are psychic dangers
to be encountered in the dark red current of thought
into which the untruthful person enters, through deceit and double-dealing. This current, which is one
of the lowest rates of vibration of all the cosmic currents surrounding the earth and mankind, contains
most of the undeveloped, disembodied souls who have
passed from earth life. These souls, by reason of
their grossness, cannot get away from the material
plane, and, through the operation of the law of attraction, are drawn by sympathy to other souls—
whether incarnated or excarnated—who are at a similar point of development. They are able now to
enjoy only by proxy, as it were, the vices from which
they are debarred by the loss of their physical bodies;
and they surround the man or woman who, by adopt-
ing vices similar to their own, have entered their
realm of thought,[1] and lead him or her to destruction;
and thus the independent sex relationist receives the
wages of ignorance. More will be said along this line
in the lecture entitled "After Death."

---

[1]The History and Power of Mind, pp. 169-177; 228-230.

LECTURE THREE.

PARENTHOOD.

Ages and ages ago, so many that it makes man dizzy to try to calculate their number, the Divine Parenthood of man began. And billions of years before man's creation, in the beginning of our Cosmic Day, God—Divine Mind—began getting the Universe—man's home—ready to receive him.

During the first great period of our Cosmic Day God—Divine Mind—desired light.[1] The command went forth: "Let there be light," and the vibrations of certain portions of the ether began to quicken and increase until, in accordance with the Divine Will, light was born. And all that was accomplished or established during the first period of our Cosmic Day was the awakening and quickening into activity of those great centers of consciousness which the Occultist calls Solar Deities or Sun Gods, the Elohim or Planetary Spirits, and the Seraphim and Cherubim.

During the second great period of our Cosmic Day, God—Divine Mind—desired that the undeveloped portion of Itself should separate from the developed portion, in order that the undeveloped portion should become subjected to evolutionary law applicable more

---

[1] The History and Power of Mind, p. 71, "Genesis."

directly to itself. "And God said, Let there be a firmament in the midst of the waters, and let it divide the waters from the waters. And God made the firmament and divided the waters which were under the firmament from the waters which were above the firmament, and it was so."

In other words, through the operation of Divine Will, the differentiated portion of Itself became separated from the undifferentiated; the manifested was separated from the unmanifested, and there appeared in the Universe two distinct portions of the Universal Consciousness which men now call mind and matter.[1]

Both of these portions were of the same substance, but differed by reason of each portion's different rate of vibrations: "And God called the firmament (the undifferentiated portion of Itself) Heaven, and the evening and the morning were the second day."

During the third great period of our Cosmic Day, God—Divine Mind—desired that from the differentiated portion of Itself there should be prepared abiding places for Its sons—when they should be created. And again the Divine Will went forth throughout the Universe and the creative Gods, the Elohim or Planetary Spirits commenced their work. Their long period of inaction during the Cosmic Night was now passed and they were ready at the first call of the Universal Consciousness to begin the labors of the new Cosmic Day.[2] "And God said, Let the waters

---

[1]The History and Power of Mind, pp. 36-37.

[2]The History and Power of Mind, pp. 101-103.

under the heaven (the differentiated portion of It-self) be gathered together unto one place and let the dry land appear, and it was so. And God called the dry land Earth (Worlds) and the gathering together of the waters called He seas, and God saw that it was good."

And all that was accomplished during the third period of our Cosmic Day was the commencement of such world forms as the Elohim or Planetary Spirits saw pictured by Divine Mind in the differentiated portion of Itself. God made the mental pictures of what It desired should be materialized during the several periods, and this mental picturing is the creation described in the first chapter of Genesis, and in the second chapter of Genesis to verse four.

The fourth great period of our Cosmic Day was one of Celestial Chaos. For at that time there was confusion in the workshop of the heavenly Gods. Many of the planetary systems were blazing masses of burning gas. Comets were flying through space, colliding and coalescing with other comets, and Divine Law and Order, during the greater part of that period, were prospective but not realized. The suns which were to become magnetic centers for world systems were blazing and bursting with the intense energy that was poured into them by the Solar Deities. The creative Gods seemed to play at cricket with comets, suns and worlds, and the whole heaven was a pyrotechnical display of flaming planets.

At the fifth great period of our Cosmic Day Divine Mind declared that harmony should again prevail in the Universe, and, in accordance with the Divine Will, celestial order came out of cosmic chaos. Planets and planetary systems became adjusted to their orbits and began revolving about their respective magnetic centers or suns, and the war of worlds came to an end. "And God said, Let the Earth (Worlds) bring forth grass, the herb yielding seed and the fruit tree yielding fruit after his kind whose seed is in itself upon the earth (worlds) and it was so." "And God said, Let the waters bring forth abundantly the moving creature that hath life, and fowl that may fly above the earth in the open firmament of heaven. And God created great whales and every living creature that moveth, which the waters brought forth abundantly after their kind, and every winged fowl after his kind, and God saw that it was good, . . . and the evening and the morning were the fifth day." The words "and God said let there be," or "God made," etc., in Genesis, always refer to the mental creation of Divine Mind.

On the morning of the sixth great period of our Cosmic Day "God made the beast of the earth after his kind, . . . and everything that creepeth upon the earth after his kind, and God saw that it was good."[1]

The mental pictures in Divine Mind not yet objectivized by the Elohim or Planetary Spirits had now to be materialized, and "these are the generations of the

---

[1]The History and Power of Mind, pp. 69-71.

heavens and of the earth when they *were* created, in
the day that the *Lord God* made the earth and the
heavens, and every plant of the field *before it was in
the earth,* and every herb of the field *before it grew,*"[1]
in accordance with the divine ideal or picture. Then
the Lord God—the Seraphim and the Cherubim—
with their tremendous united power, became the
demonstrators and brought these pictures into objectivity, or, "formed (animal) man of the dust of the
ground . . . and out of the *ground* made the Lord God
to grow every tree . . . and out of the *ground* the Lord
God formed every beast of the field and every fowl of
the air." This was the second or physical creation described in the second chapter of Genesis, and which
is elaborated in lecture four.

And when at last everything was ready to receive
mankind, "God said, Let us make man in our image,
after our likeness; and let them have dominion over
the fish of the sea, and over the fowl of the air and
over the cattle, and over all the earth, and over every
creeping thing that creepeth upon the earth." With
Divine Mind's desire for parenthood there came into
the Universal Consciousness the mental pictures of
the Sons of God; and when the Elohim saw those pictures they commenced to draw individual portions of
Divine Mind from the differentiated part of God
and moulding each portion into an oval or egg-
shaped form, like themselves, they fulfilled the com-

---

[1] The italics are our own and are to emphasize the occult meaning of
the passage.

mand and created each son in their own "image" and after their own likeness."[1] Then they gave to each ego its own rate of vibration; and the magnetic power inherent in each, because of its Divine origin, made it an independent, magnetic, evolving, immortal mind, through whom its Father, Divine Mind, would be able to express Itself; and through whom It would be able to raise to a higher point of development the vegetable and animal kingdoms below man. And it was for this purpose that God gave His sons dominion over the earth and over all it contained: For Divine Mind works only through individual centers, from the Solar Deities, the highest and greatest, down to the smallest and most insignificant creature in the Universe.

When the Sons of God incarnated in the animal forms of earth they immediately began using the laws which govern procreation. In those ancient days men knew no more about gestation than they did about digestion and became parents more from animal impulse than from any desire for offspring. In their ignorance of the law they not only used, but they also abused, it; and yet, unconsciously to themselves, they became instruments, though many times imperfect ones, for the Divine Mind, their Father to work through. But God is patient with Its children, and after many ages of ignorance had passed, with their attendant suffering, man reached a point in his evolution where he recognized that there was a higher

---

[1]The History of Power and Mind, pp. 65-68.

power than his own, and began to have a desire for a knowledge concerning it.

He wanted to know the truth about himself and about his relationship to that power. He also recognized the fact that there were laws which governed him and his environment and he desired to become acquainted with them.. Before the awakening of his desire to know the truth concerning his family relations, his children had been born with the regularity of the coming of the seasons. Sometimes there were so many that he could scarcely get food for himself and for them. And when hunger commenced to gnaw daily he suddenly awoke to the realization of the truth that he had been extravagant in exercising his parental privileges, and, notwithstanding his race belief that man should be fruitful and multiply and replenish the earth, he began to think about retrenching and demanded in his heart to know the laws governing the conception and birth of children and how to regulate the size of his family.

The law of demand and supply has been operating in the Universe since it was created. And although men have not known how to use that law intelligently and scientifically, still, whatsoever a man desires in his heart will come to him sooner or later. After a long period of wishing and waiting, man's desire for knowledge concerning conception and parental duty was met. Advanced egos, men who had lived through a former period of evolution and had gained a knowledge far beyond that of the people whom they came to help, were sent to this earth to incarnate in human form and to become teachers of the rising, growing races.

As the cool and gentle dew from heaven falls upon the parched and feverish earth, refreshing and reviving it after the burning rays of the sun have disappeared, so did the wisdom brought to ignorant, suffering mankind, by the Teachers of Occult Truths, revive and encourage such egos as were ready to receive it. These Teachers taught men and women that to become the father or mother of a human body was a sacred, divine privilege; that parenthood should always be assumed with deepest reverence and with an earnest demand for wisdom to train each little personality in a manner that would make it tractable for the incarnating ego to control; that when the tiny brain should become expanded to the point where the ego could take full possession it would be a good instrument, instead of a poor one, for it to use. As the Creative Gods in the heavens moulded the minds of men into forms similar to their own, so do the animal men of earth now reproduce their forms in those of their children.

It is true that "fools rush in where angels fear to tread," and the advanced egos see with regret the consequences which must come to the men and women who carelessly and recklessly assume the responsibilities of parenthood and then deliberately shirk those responsibilities, or turn their little ones over to the care of ignorant and viciously inclined persons.

If a beautiful and wonderful jewel, a thing so rare that there was but one other like it in the Universe, were to be presented to a woman, would she give that jewel to a hireling to wear? Would she carelessly leave it, with its beauty and purity unguarded, for weeks and perhaps for months, to be smirched and defiled by those to whom she has entrusted it, and who know or care nothing for its value? What would the world think of the King who gave his crown to his valet to do with as he saw fit? And yet, in comparison with the soul jewels in the crown of parenthood, those in the crown of a monarch are most insignificant.

Before a woman conceives the embryo which is to become a human body, the Divine Law attracts to her an ego, who in a past life has been associated either pleasantly or unpleasantly with her or with the man who will be the father of her child. Sometimes this ego, who is about to reincarnate, does not leave her for weeks, and perhaps for months, before conception. It is ever present, waiting for the moment to come when copulation will occur and the conditions will be favorable for the conception of its body. And when the desired conditions are produced it sends forth itself into the ovum within the mother, a tiny, blue, magnetic thread and fastens it to the life germ which the father has just deposited there.

To the spiritual eyes of the Seer this magnetic thread appears upon the subjective plane as the web thread of the spider appears to physical eyes upon the material plane. Both seem to be equally fragile and easily broken; but the magnetic thread, when once attached to its embryo, is strengthened in its hold by the reincarnating ego's intense desire for life. The Law of Attraction which brought that ego to that family also gives protection to the embryo through its action upon the uterus containing it. It causes that organ to contract around the tiny life germ for the first few days after it is received, or until a membrane, which will be a further protection to the embryo, is completely formed within the opening of the cervix.

When conception is established, then comes the building of the body which the reincarnating ego will possess. If the ego or builder is an undeveloped mind and is being forced back without its volition into earth-life by the great Law, then the building of its body is not a conscious creation of its own, but is the result of the physical action of the law and of the mother's mind.

But the advanced ego consciously selects from the mother's blood the finest atoms for its embryo, and mentally moulds its vehicle according to its purpose. The reincarnating ego completely envelopes the mother of its embryo at the moment of conception and continues in that close relationship during the whole period of gestation, and effects more or less her disposition and desires. If it is of a weaker nature than hers, then its influence is not externally apparent to any large degree; but if it is a stronger, even if it be of a more undeveloped nature than hers, it dominates her in every way. She will no longer have the same likes or dislikes, will sometimes yield to the most unaccountable tastes, and often to depraved appetites. Persons whom she once loved she will now despise or vice versa. Sometimes she will seem to be obsessed by a demon of animal passion and during the whole period of gestation her sexual desires will be insatiable. To her friends she becomes a source of sorrow and disappointment, because they do not understand the cause of the change in her. She, herself, may not understand it, and usually does not care to know the reason.

If she were to be examined psychically by a clairvoyant she would be seen surrounded and completely enveloped by a dark shadow—which is the aura of the ego who is incarnating as her child; and its colors would seem to have entirely overcome and suppressed her own. During the period of gestation perhaps she would be obsessed or insane—as obsession is more popularly called.

Through the intense and perhaps gross desires of the reincarnating ego, it may impress the tiny body with impurities. It may poison the blood of the child with its own hatred and anger. Through its uncontrolled emotions and passions it often produces an abnormal condition of some of its internal organs, and the body will be born with impure blood and a defective brain, or perhaps with a physical deformity of limb or of body. Then it would be said that these misfortunes were inherited from its parents, or that they were birthmarks caused by some fault of the mother, or by some mishap which befell her during the period of gestation.

When the woman is relieved of the burden of carrying the child and her normal, mental condition has reasserted itself, by reason of the fact that the reincarnating ego has been removed a step from her aura, she often suffers the deepest remorse because of the unfortunate plight of her child. Her friends, and perhaps her husband, tell her how disgracefully she has misbehaved, and blame her for the condition of her offspring. In reality, however, she neither consciously nor unconsciously produced it, and it may be that the ego of the child was drawn into her family because of its past relationship with her husband, who is now its father.

It is true that she was karmically connected with her husband and that the Law brought them together for that reason. Through her relationship with him she had to participate in his karma, but she may not have had a past association with the particular ego who was now reincarnated as their child, and should not be blamed for its misfortunes.

Some one may ask why is it not right, under such circumstances, to produce a miscarriage and dislodge the undesirable embryo, rather than to permit it to develop into an unruly and disreputable individual and to become a source of trouble to its parents. To such a question the Occultist would reply: Nothing whatever would be gained by producing such a mis-carriage, since that unruly, undeveloped ego actually belongs to that family by reason of past association, and the law must continue to bring it back again and again until that woman or man to whom it belonged is compelled to give it parentage, and thus pay the debt that he or she owes to it. For all mankind at this point in the evolution of the race owe debts that can be paid in no other way than by becoming parents, and the Divine Law is an inexorable collector of karmic debts.

If a developed or advanced ego is seeking reincarnation in a certain family it is also because of karmic reasons.[1] During some past life there was formed a pleasant relationship between it and some member of that family. Or perhaps it may be that it is the other half of the ego of the mother to whom it has now come in the relationship of child.[2] In a case like this that mother will be uplifted during the entire period of gestation and she will anticipate the coming of her child with the happiness that she would feel at the prospect of a visit from her dearest friend. She will dream of it at night and plan beautiful things for it by day. It will be a pleasure to her to fashion the dainty garments that it will wear, and perhaps she will not permit them to be made by other hands than her own. Things happening in her household or among her friends which once disturbed and annoyed

---

[1] Mata the Magician, p. 154.

[2] Linked Lives, p. 203.

her now bring a smile to her face. She is permeated with the aura of the ego that she loves better than any other in the Universe and her sacred picture grows daily clearer to her mental vision. This is because it has come so near; it has indeed become a part of her and is blended with her as it was before they came to earth to suffer and grow strong.

If the incarnating ego is not the other half of herself, but is equal to her in development, then she may be contented and pleased with the possibility of becoming a mother. If it should be an ego greatly in advance of her, she would be blessed in many ways by the close relationship during gestation and the impetus she would receive from the association would carry her a long step in advance of where she was when she conceived the little body.[1]

Heredity, according to the common acceptance of the term, is impossible. Neither the father nor the mother of a child can give to it its character or any part of it. It is true that if the reincarnating ego is not as strong as either of its parents the physical body may resemble in appearance one or both of them. This may be due to one of two causes: First the reincarnating ego may, in a general way, be of a similar character to one or both parents; or it may be that it is not a conscious builder of its body and negatively waits for the Law and for its mother's mind to mould the body for it.

By many physicians, and by society in general, it

---

[1] Mata the Magician, p. 105.

is believed that the father or mother can transmit impurities and disease through their blood to their innocent offspring, and that a child will thus be made to suffer for the sins of its parents. The Occultist would say that no ego could reincarnate with parents who would transmit poisons or disease to its body, unless, by reason of its own past mistakes, that ego deserved to have them. It could never be brought into that family by the Law, if it did not belong there, because the Law. is Justice. To the mother who finds in her children the taint of a poison which she knows she did not give them, but which came from their father, the Occultist would say: Because of this let no bitterness live in your heart toward the man whom you have espoused, because it is a debt which is being paid and the child whom you believe to be an inno- cent sufferer for another's sins had sins of its own to expiate and is expiating them now under the right and proper conditions.

By this it is not meant that nothing should be done to improve the condition of the child, because im- provement is always needed at every moment during the life of a human being. But God should not be blamed for the affliction, neither should it be believed that it is an especial dispensation of Providence.[1] Force should not be wasted by weeping and lament- ing, but rather should be used to help that ego to live a better life than it did before, in order that it may not suffer again in a like manner. And while

[1]The History and Power of Mind, pp. 116-119; 244.

the poison is being eliminated from the child's body, the poisonous thoughts which produced the condition should also be eliminated from its mind.

There are sins of omission as well as sins of commission, and nowhere in any walk of life are there more of these to be found than in the relationship of parenthood. The mother who is too ignorant or too careless to watch her baby and prevent that little animal personality from contracting in its infancy the habits which will later lead to sexual abuses, wakens some day to the realizing sense that her beloved son or daughter, in whom her heart's pride is centered, has become a nervous, physical wreck because of the fearful practice of masturbation; or, perhaps, has entered the broad road of prostitution.

Modesty is the first lesson that should be taught to the baby. When it begins to toddle teach it that there are certain portions of its body which must always be kept decorously covered, and which must not be handled or played with. Bad impressions are often made upon a baby's mind by the admiring mother who bares its little body and shows it to her friends, or has its picture taken in its nudity. Baby soon learns to believe that nudity is nice, and it is more difficult for it to unlearn a thing than to learn it.

When a baby girl has reached the age of understanding, the wise mother will win her confidence by talking with her alone each day upon the subjects which seem of the greatest interest to the child. She will ask her questions concerning the children with whom she plays, and about the servants in the house who have the care of her; and very soon she will be able to determine something of the daily influences which are brought to bear upon the child. During those hours of sacred confidence the plastic mind of the child should be moulded into the right condition to resist the evil of the outside world. If during those precious talks the mother teaches her that she is never alone, but is surrounded by night as well as by day by Divine Consciousness which knows every thought she thinks and every act that she performs, the child will not easily be led into transgression.

Before the girl reaches puberty, the time when the progressed reincarnating ego usually takes full possession of its body,[1] the wise mother will impress upon her mind that for the protection of her good name, and in order that her future husband should fully trust in her virtue and purity, God created within her body a hymen, which is the physical expression of the purity of her thoughts. She will tell her that this expression of physical purity must be guarded as carefully as her eyes, which are but the material windows for her soul. And she will impress the thought upon the girl's mind that the hymen is a veil for the sacred creative organs within her body, and it must remain where God placed it until the time shall come when she will enter into the relationship of wife.

Because of her sex the baby girl should not be made

---

[1] Mata the Magician, p. 126.

an isolated subject to be taught the necessity for purity of thought and action. The baby boy should begin his private interviews with his mother at an equally tender age. For it is a great mistake to believe that because he is a boy he does not need to be taught purity or does not come under the same rules that should govern the conduct of his sister. Egos are sexless and incarnate alternately in male and female personalities. It is the mind of the boy that the mother is educating, and it matters not which sex it uses, the truth and purity which it is taught to-day will last throughout its future incarnations.

It is a mistake to believe that the modest man is not a strong character, or that he is a weakling because he refuses to enter into the follies and vices which society sanctions and condones. So let not the mothers be afraid of robbing their sons of any of the majesty of their manhood by teaching them along the same lines that they teach their daughters. Virtue is a wonderous jewel and shines as brightly in the crown of manhood as in that of womanhood. And in whichever place it may be it always serves as a strong light to illumine the pathway of its possessor on the journey of life.

The Occultist would say, be not ashamed to be or to become a modest, truthful, virtuous man; for by so doing you will be entitled to instruction in the highest wisdom given to man upon this planet. But if you have not the rock foundation of virtue and truth to stand upon you can not bear to know the highest

Occult teachings, which are given only to those who are thus prepared and are therefore ready.

Teaching by word of mouth is not the only parental duty. The lessons taught the child as it sits on the parent's knee are beautiful and impressive, but they do not do all the work that is needed in the child's heart garden. There is the daily example which both parents put before it and which goes very far toward moulding the little one's character into a perfect or imperfect image of manhood or womanhood.

It is natural and right that the mother should be the child's ideal of perfect womanhood, and that the father should be its ideal of perfect manhood. It is also natural that those ideals should be raised or lowered in the child's mind according to the behavior of the objects of those ideals. How can a mother teach modesty to a child who sees her exposing her own person in a state of nudity? How can she teach her child purity of thought and action when she, herself, indulges in impurity? She may think she is concealing her conduct from her child, but those little bright eyes see much more than she imagines, and that active little mind will draw its own conclusions at a very tender age. How can a mother teach a child to be truthful when she, herself, tells falsehoods to it and before it? It is true that children are often impelled to ask embarrassing questions, and desire to know many things which it may not seem advisable to answer at the time. In such cases, instead of telling a falsehood to conceal the truth, it is better to say:

"When you are old enough to be told this thing which you are asking about, I will answer your question."

If a child of five or six years wishes to know where her baby brother came from, it is neither advisable nor necessary to enter into a detailed account of the circumstances and conditions which brought him into the family. But the little one's question being an honest one, deserves a respectful and considerate reply; and it is not right to put her off with the usual tale of a stork or a fairy bringing and leaving him on the doorstep; nor that the doctor took him out of his box where he keeps all other babies. If it does not seem advisable to tell the truth then, one should promise to explain the mystery at some future time.

It is a mistake to tell children the Santa Claus falsehood. It is true that it makes a very pretty story, and a child lives in a delightful dream of expectation until the sad day comes when it learns the truth. The awakening is usually a terrible shock and disappointment, and its confidence is forever shaken in the person who told and maintained the falsehood. Circumstances which seem trifling and unimportant to a parent are of great importance to the child who is learning its first lessons in life. And the little one's disappointments are as hard for it to bear as are those which break the hearts and ruin the lives of men and women.

Because of their love for their children, parents often make slaves of themselves and sacrifice much which they need and desire, in order that their children may have more than they can afford to give them. It is not an unusual thing to hear a mother say: "I will never see my daughter's hands look as mine do. She shall never work as I have worked if I can help it. My child shall have all the advantages that were denied to me because of the poverty of my parents. It is my duty to deny myself in order that she may become accomplished."

The one object in life is the development and growth of every individual ego, and not one should be retarded in its evolution by becoming the slave of another. The mother who works all day in the kitchen, laundry, or at household work, in order to save her daughter's white hands from the stains of labor, is not only retarding her own growth, but she is at the same time fostering in her daughter's character a degree of selfishness which will retard instead of advance her progress in life. If the ego who came to reincarnate as the daughter of the hard-working, self-sacrificing woman had not needed and deserved the lessons in physical labor which Divine Law intended she should get in that environment, then she would not have been brought to that family to incarnate. And the mother, through her mistaken sense of duty, transgresses against the Divine Law when she refuses to share her labors with her child. Because of the many self-imposed tasks the mother cannot take time to read or to think along educational lines; she has very little or no time to spend upon her toilet, and as a consequence she appears illiterate, stupid and poorly gowned. The daughter for whom she has toiled is ashamed of her, and perhaps repudiates her relationship if an opportunity is presented.

There is a saying that if a man makes a doormat of himself his friends will wipe their shoes on him. This is a very terse way of stating a great truth and applies to the case under discussion. This mother earns the punishment she receives for attempting to evade the operation of the Law which governs her own and her daughter's progress. The punishment is bestowed upon her through the individual whom she, by her mistaken ideas of duty, has retarded in her development. It is a fearful thing to hinder the evolution of another ego, and never fails to bring its punishment.

It is not infrequent that the father and mother are left unthanked and alone to toil and pay off the mortgage that, while laboring under their mistaken sense of duty, they put upon their home in order that their boy could go to college and have a sufficient amount of money to spend in company with the wealthy men's sons with whom he would associate during his college days. And it is not infrequent, when the young man returns to his humble home and compares it and his parents with the homes and parents of his fashionable friends, that he feels ashamed and aggrieved and often blames his father and mother for his poverty. Such a young man might be heard to say: "They brought me into the world against my will and now they may take care of me," and the disappointed

father and mother bow their heads and bend their
backs under the burden which their mistaken sense
of duty put upon them.

It was not the duty of those parents to risk losing
their home to give their son an opportunity in life
which neither of them could have. But it was their
duty to share with him their labors as well as their
blessings. If the boy had an aspiration for a college
course, and was willing to earn the money to pay for
it, they had no right to keep him at home or to refuse
him the opportunity to progress along any line he
chose to follow. Because he was their son they had
no right to demand a lifelong servitude from him any
more than, because they gave him birth, he had the
right to demand a life servitude from them. There
were experiences which he needed in that humble environment which would serve to bring out the strong
points in his character as no other environment could;
and Divine Mind placed him there because it was the
best place for him to be. It was not necessary, however, that he should always remain in that environment, and after the necessary lessons had been
learned and the required strength gained, he had the
right to release himself and to work out his life problems in any way that he liked best.

It is not an unusual thing to hear a mother say:
"My daughter must have jewels and fine clothes and
be 'up to date'; it does not matter about me, I am
getting old, and an old woman does not need anything anyway."

This is another case of mistaken parental duty. In order that their daughter may have fine clothes, jewels and be "up to date," an evolving ego creeps into a corner and hides herself because of her shabby, old-fashioned appearance. She cannot meet her daughter's friends because she has given everything she possessed toward ornamenting and beautifying her daughter. She does not know what kind of society her daughter meets because she is not permitted to appear in the parlor when company is present. The real maternal duty of supervising the selection of her daughter's friends is overruled by the mistaken duty of keeping her "up to date," and permitting her to try to force herself into a social position which the family exchequer does not warrant, without sacrifice to the parents.

The mother's punishment for her transgression of the Law frequently comes in the form of dishonor to the daughter and a consequent disgrace to the family name; and she is compelled to creep further than ever into the background and hide her head for shame of that which she has been instrumental in precipitating upon herself and upon her child.

When the majority of the women of any nation refuse to become mothers, whether it is because of poverty and inability to support children, or because they are too fashionable and have not the time to give to the sacred duties of motherhood, then the world may know that "race suicide" has begun in that portion of the globe. For the law of demand and supply works along this line as forcefully as along any other, and when women commence to picture themselves as barren and demand barrenness, they are scientifically creating that condition for themselves and for the nation to which they belong. If artificial means are used to produce this condition the demise of the nation will be hastened. And if a point has been reached where its limitation of thought, its fixed religious beliefs and its unprogressive modes of living are causing mental strangulation to the individuals who compose it, then the addition of these various causes to the first great cause soon brings national demolition.

For example, take the Chinese race. There are a few individuals in that great nation who manifest a desire to break through the ancient customs of their ancestors by going to America or elsewhere to live. Some of these immigrants adopt, to a limited extent, the customs and modes of living of the people among whom they go. But as a nation the Chinese are bound by their religious beliefs to the time of Confucius; and because of their ancestral worship cannot depart from their ancient religious customs. Some of the men who come to America pretend to manifest an interest in the religions of their adopted country; but, as has been repeatedly shown, there is no foundation for that interest other than curiosity or a desire for gain.

With most of their men and with many of their women sex relationship has reached a point of utter moral depravity. Licentious indulgences are with them a recreation and a pastime. Many of their women are born barren and, in order that prostitution among them may not be restrained by child-bearing, many women are made barren by artificial means. This last-named crime alone would destroy the nation after a few more generations. But when that crime is combined with all the limitations and obstructions which its people have put in the way of their own evolution, there is but one result that can come and that is destruction of the entire Chinese nation.

It is to be hoped that the people of our own and other nations, who believe themselves to be progressive and enlightened, may learn through observation something of the causes and unmistakable signs which precede and produce race suicide, and not be so blind as to require experiences, similar to those of a dying nation, in order to learn the lesson Divine Law is trying to teach.

Since there are two sides to every subject, there is another side to this one. In opposition to race suicide stands the other extreme, which is parental slavery. Parenthood is a necessary experience in man's evolution, but parental slavery, produced by overmuch parenthood, is another great mistake. Because God said on the morning of man's creation "be fruitful and multiply and replenish the earth and subdue it," many people have believed it to be a duty they owed to God to give birth to as many children as possible, and regardless of health or of financial conditions have borne children in such numbers that they have been utterly unable to take care of them. This is exhibiting an extravagance in the parental privileges of man and is as much to be deplored as any other extravagance.

It is true that there are many egos upon the subjective plane awaiting an opportunity for re-incarnation. But so there is an abundance of food in the world waiting to be transformed into blood, bone and muscle. A man who would constantly overcrowd his stomach in order to accommodate the food that was waiting to be transformed into something higher than food would be abusing that organ and would soon reach a point where he could not retain any food, and he would shorten his life as a penalty for his extravagance in eating.

There are certain religious orders which encourage and even command their female members to give birth to as many children as possible; and priests have been known to advise the sacrifice of the life of a mother for the sake of bringing another child into the world, even though at that moment there was a family of little ones to be left motherless by his decision.

The Occultist would say that such advise as this, coming from a priest, supposedly a holy man, should be regarded as a crime, and should be made punishable by the State. It is a mistake to allow men to teach ignorant people to commit such wrongs as these, for it is as great a wrong to sacrifice the incarnation of one ego for the sake of giving incarnation to another as it is to take life in any other way.

It is not necessary that an ego should become a slave to a larger family of children than it has means to provide for comfortably. It is not right nor just for a man and a woman to toil early and late and be deprived of the advantages and pleasures of life in order that a number of other egos may have an opportunity to reincarnate. But every married man and woman should be willing to pay the parental debt they owe to the Divine Law, by having some children. In other words, they should be willing and glad to give bodies and to educate at least two other egos in payment for their own birth and education.

But if an individual does not wish to pay his debt and prefers to shirk his sacred obligation; if he feels either mentally or physically unqualified for parenthood, then he should refuse to marry and should devote his time to the improvement of his mental and physical condition and toward helping to improve the condition of others who need his assistance.

The Nazarene said: "For ye have the poor always with you," and the man or woman who does not desire to marry and become a parent can find much to do for the fatherless and motherless children in the world.

LECTURE FOUR.

PHYSICAL AND PSYCHIC DEVELOPMENT.

In the three preceding lectures there have been a few brief references to cosmogonal evolution and to the relationship existing between God—Divine Mind—and some of the greatest individualized centers of force in the Universe; such as the Solar Deities and the Elohim or Creative Gods. It must be understood that these great Centers of Consciousness were the evolutionary products of remote Cosmic Days, having evolved from manhood into godhood, and that on the morning of our first period they were called again into activity and were not newly created as was anciently believed. For God did not create the earth and all it contained first and then make "two great lights: the greater light to rule the day and the lesser light to rule the night: and the stars and set them in the firmament of the heaven to give light upon the Earth," as is stated in the first chapter of Genesis.

But, in accordance with the Divine Law, which is also the law of necessity, the stronger centers of force preceded the weaker, in this Cosmic Day, the same as they did in previous periods, and will forever continue to do; and therefore the Occultist would say, before the creation of worlds, or of planetary systems, the suns were created which were to give light and heat and magnetic life to those worlds. These orbs were created by the greatest individualized centers of consciousness who exist in the Universe, the Solar Deities—commonly called Sun Gods by sun-worshipping peoples. And after those centers of magnetic force and light had been created and their orbits established, the Elohim or Planetary Spirits, brought into materialized form lesser magnetic centers and arranged them into systems of worlds.

On the morning of the fifth period of our Cosmic Day, Celestial Beings, who in our Scripture were sometimes called the Seraphim and Cherubim, and who had been but waiting for the Divine Summons to arouse them to activity began the work which the All Father, Divine Mind, desired them to do.

Like the Elohim, these great Beings were also centers of individualized consciousness, but differed from them in being the products of the Cosmic Day preceding this. When the last Cosmic Night came on they had, through individualization, evolved to a point beyond the probability of re-absorbment into the Universal Consciousness.[1] And although they were possessed of lesser power, being smaller centers than the Elohim, still the individual Godhood of each had been established, and they belonged to the "Heavenly Host" who work everlastingly for the up-building of the Universe.

Throughout our Scripture these Beings are fre-

---

[1] The History and Power of Mind, pp. 100-101.

quently mentioned, and were called by various names, according to the impression made upon the mind of the individual who saw them. Usually they appeared singly to persons, as in the case of Saul, who was going to Damascus to persecute the Christians. The description he gave of the Being who stopped him in his mad career was more nearly correct than was usually given in those days. He was impressed with the thought that it was Jesus of Nazareth who spoke to him, and in the report of the incident it is said: "Suddenly there shined round about him a light from heaven; and he fell to the earth and heard a voice saying unto him, Saul, Saul, why persecutest thou me?" and for three days afterward he was without sight, and neither ate nor drank.

It may or may not have been the Being who had been using the body of the humble Nazarene in order to teach humanity how to live up to higher standards of morality; but whether it was He or not, it certainly was a Celestial Being who had been sent to Saul to enlighten him regarding the mistakes he was making in persecuting his fellowmen. And it was not the first nor the last incident of the kind which has occurred among mankind.

In the first chapter of Ezekiel there is a most graphic description of four of these Beings who, the prophet declared, had appeared to him. He said they looked exactly alike and had "the appearance of the likeness of the glory of the Lord." And when he heard the voice of the One who spoke, he fell upon his face and was unable to stand before that holy company.

It is not unreasonable to believe that the description of that Celestial Quartet given by Ezekiel was highly colored by his intense emotional condition, as well as by the imperfection of his clairvoyant vision at that time. So far as the details are concerned, his description could not have been correct, since Beings, who have reached the point of development which entitles them to the position of Creative Gods, have no need for wings, neither do they have animal heads nor bird faces. But they are great Souls who in their Cosmic Day were men like the men of our present day, but who have now become disembodied, yet have retained every principle except their physical vehicle, for which they have no further need. And, instead of going to some far-away heaven and spending an eternity in selfish bliss, they have chosen to do the work of self-sacrifice which ends only with the Cosmic Day in which that work is undertaken. Combined they form the invisible "Host" which ever protects and watches over humanity within its karmic limits. Singly or in pairs, they sometimes visit individuals who have become worthy of their help. They are the protecting, compassionate, guardian angels for struggling, suffering souls of earth. They are the Elder Brothers, the Saviours, the Avatars for undeveloped men.

With their intense and rapid rates of vibration they sometimes appear to man as great centers of

light or as radiant suns encircled by all the colors
of the rainbow. And if one of these wondrous Beings
comes into close proximity with an undeveloped incarnated ego, that person is often unable to bear the
Presence and retain his consciousness on the material
plane.

Sometimes one of these Beings takes a physical
body and uses it for a short time for the purpose of
enabling Him to mingle with men and thus help a
race or a nation by leading it over a difficult place in
its evolution.

But whether incarnated or not, they inspire and
uplift the leaders of peoples, teaching them at all
times the highest truths that they are able to understand.

The laws operating in the macrocosm also control
the microcosm, and since in order to evolve, Divine
Mind has to express Itself through the instrumen-
tality of individualized centers, it was necessary in
the sixth period of our Cosmic Day, after suns and
worlds and systems of worlds had been created, that
It should continue further with the individualization
of Itself. After the earth was formed and adjusted
to its orbit in the heavens, and when its surface had
become sufficiently cooled and encrusted to form a
substantial foundation, the vapors which had been
accumulating in its surrounding atmosphere, by reason of the intense heat emanating from it as a mass
of burning gases, were precipitated back upon it in
the form of a heavy rain. This is described in Genesis

second chapter and sixth verse: "But there went up a mist from the earth and watered the whole face of the ground." The Occultist further says that there was a great downpour of rain which lasted for many years until the whole face of the earth was covered with water. And that for ages Mother Earth was covered with the restless, surging sea.[1]

When the time had come in the earth's evolution that individualized life could be maintained upon it, the earth, through its own magnetic power of attraction, commenced to draw from the differentiated portion of the Universal Consciousness surrounding it the cosmic life currents which were to ensoul it and to ensoul all the animal forms which it should sometime produce. The first current which was attracted, and which entirely permeated it, was the cosmic current orange. This is the current that gives life to everything and without which neither minerals nor vegetables nor animals could exist.[2] Without its renewing power even the earth itself would soon become a huge ball of crumbling coke and slowly disintegrate. After the life current was established and had formed a broad protecting band around the earth then came the cosmic current red[3] and blended with the orange upon its outer edge. In this current are the elements which induce procreation and therefore it was a necessary force to aid in the work of reproduction

---

[1] From Incarnation to Re-incarnation, p. 8.

[2] The History and Power of Mind, p. 231.

[3] The History and Power of Mind, p. 228.

of the vegetable and animal forms on earth.   After the cosmic current red then came another which vibrates at the rate producing green[2] and blended with the red upon its outer edge.   In this current are the elements which produce and maintain the principle of individualization, and thus it was also a necessary factor in the work which Divine Mind desired done upon the earth.

When our globe had become surrounded and ensouled with these currents or colors it was ready to bring forth into objectivity the various vegetable and animal forms which Divine Mind had created on the mental plane, and in this work the Seraphim and Cherubim, the Lord Gods of the second chapter of Genesis, became the demonstrators.[3]

According to the command of God—Divine Mind —the Elohim had created the Sons of God out of the differentiated part of the Universal Consciousness and had placed them in a realm of innocence upon another sphere or orb in our planetary chain; and now the Seraphim and Cherubim undertook the work of creating the forms of vegetable and animal life and the bodies of animal men out of that part of the differentiated portion of the Universal Consciousness which had been attracted to and had ensouled the earth.

Since Divine Mind had pictured certain portions of the earth covered with grasses, flowers and trees,

---

[2]The History and Power of Mind, p. 232.

[3]From Incarnation to Re-Incarnation, p. 63.

and had thus formed the matrices for these individualized expressions of Itself, seven Seraphs and seven Cherubs, half souls of each other, formed into a group of Creative Beings for the purpose of materializing Divine Mind's mental creations. These Beings with their united force raised continents above the surface of the waters and caused "the waters under the heaven to be gathered together unto one place." Then they slowly drew from the orange, the red and the green currents, ensouling the earth, a combined force which, as it passed through the mineralized soil and appeared upon its surface, individualized and materialized into the many forms of vegetable life which they had seen pictured in Divine Mind "before they grew."

First came the tiny lichens upon the rocks, then the grass and flowers, the shrubs and finally the trees; and thus the command of God—Divine Mind—was fulfilled; "and out of the ground" made the Lord Gods to grow every plant of the field and every "tree that is pleasant for the sight, and good for food."

After the vegetable kingdom was created and was ready to support the animal life that was to come, then this group of Celestial Beings began slowly to materialize the pictures they saw in Divine Mind of the fish. First came the various kinds of mussels, mollusks and bivalves. All were without shells in the beginning but afterward, those that needed, evolved such protection as would preserve life and maintain continued existence. And after ages and ages there were evolved from the mussel, fish; and from the fish a creature half fish and half fowl, which finally evolved to fowl and flew above the waters instead of swam in the waters, and thus was fulfilled the mandate of Divine Mind: "Let the waters bring forth abundantly the moving creature that hath life, and fowl that may fly above the earth in the open firmament of heaven."

And after the waters had been made to bring forth, then these Celestial Beings began slowly to materialize the insect and animal forms which they had seen pictured in Divine Mind. From the decaying roots of the grasses and the flowers the life principle was drawn into tiny insect and animal forms (which of course did not include the malignant creatures which were subsequently the offspring of men's minds).' And from the decaying roots of shrubs and trees the life principle was drawn into larger animal forms.

The soul of the squirrel which now has its home in the hollow of a decaying tree was once the soul of a tree. Then it depended upon the soil and the atmosphere for its individual maintenance and its limitations held it firmly attached to the mother earth which bore it. When its experience as a tree had been sufficient, and when its material tree body began to decay, the Universal Consciousness, desiring a higher individualization for it, acted as the evolutionary impulse and pushed the tree soul out of its dying vehicle, and the Celestial Beings moulded it into the tiny

---

'The History and Power of Mind, p. 173.

squirrel form which they saw pictured in Divine Mind. Because of its former life as a tree and because of its past associations with the forest, in its new and more progressed form it loved and made its home among the trees, until after many re-incarnations as a squirrel it outgrew that condition also and was able to use a larger and a stronger body. And thus the animal kingdom was gradually evolved through the re-embodiment of the life principle, combined with the procreative and individualizing forces, until a form was evolved which stood erect and walked upon two feet. This form the Celestial Beings—the Lord Gods—created (evolved) from "the dust of the ground." It was the materialized and mineralized product of the earth. And when they "breathed into his nostrils the breath of life," or drew into his body the combined cosmic life currents (animal), "man became a living (animal) soul," and was ready to receive the divine, immortal principle which was waiting upon another planet to come and immortalize his existence.

In Lecture One it was shown how the Sons of God incarnated in the animal forms which the Celestial Beings had prepared for them,[1] and the account of that incarnation will not be repeated. It is sufficient to say that after the union of the two minds, the higher and the lower, or the subjective and the objective, the struggle for the supremacy commenced

---

[1] From Incarnation to Re-incarnation, p. 10; The History and Power of Mind, pp. 69-71.

between them; and although man has lived upon this planet until more than one-half of the time has passed which was allotted to his evolution, the struggle between his two minds is still strong and he is now only just beginning to learn something about his origin and nature.

Since history began to be written there have been individuals who have stood forth during their age or generation in the position of psychics; and because of the mental or moral undevelopment of some of those individuals, psychism has suffered a great deal of opprobrium. The Century Dictionary defines psychism as: "The doctrine that there is a fluid diffused throughout all nature, animating equally all living and organized beings, and that the difference which appears in their actions comes of their particular organization."

To the ordinary student this definition is confusing. For if there is a fluid diffused throughout all nature which animates equally all living and organized beings, why should not every being be equally affected by it? It also defines the word psyche, from which psychism is derived, as a Greek word meaning among other things "the human soul, spirit or mind." If it is the human soul which is supposed to be diffused throughout all nature and which animates equally all living and organized beings, then the first definition is wrong, because, as is most apparent, it is the soul's own personality which is most animated, and other beings or personalities are affected by it according to its condition of development and conse-quent influence over them.

The great trouble with the definition as it stands is, that the person who wrote it was not acquainted with the subject about which he was writing, and the trouble with humanity is that it knows very little about the subject, and is always suspicious of that with which it is not acquainted.

Occultism teaches that psychic development is soul growth and that it is not an "especial gift from God," to one individual more than to another; but it is the result of the soul's envolvement and consequent ability to see or to be otherwise conscious on planes other than the material, while it still functions in a physical body. That psychism pertains to and is an attribute of the animal soul or objective mind and not of the spirit or subjective mind is shown by the fact that many animals are psychic. There are many instances on record of horses who have been frightened at disembodied entities and have refused to draw a vehicle containing the dead body of a man or of a beast. This was because they saw or were conscious of the disembodied soul of the corpse which they feared. And dogs have been known to fear or to follow and obey the will of a disembodied ego who was invisible to persons not psychic; and yet no one could possibly claim spirituality for the animals.

The cult which is called by its followers spiritualism has had much to do with bringing confusion in the minds of investigators along this line of thought.

Many persons believe themselves to be "spiritualists," because they have accepted as a truth the fact that there is eternal progression for the human soul—which belief is an entirely separate and distinct thing from a knowledge of spirit or of things spiritual. Every living thing is animated by a soul and this soul, whether it is of a plant or of an animal or of a man, is the evolutionary force within, which re-incarnates again and again until sometime and somewhere it reaches the spiritual plane of development. Then and not until then can it be properly called spiritual.

There are two kinds of psychic development, the prudent, which leads to independent clairvoyance and clairaudience; and the imprudent, which leads to the destruction of the physical body or to insanity. The prudent psychic develops his body by living a natural, orderly life. Through meditation and concentration and by a conscious use of the life currents and of the higher cosmic currents, he keeps his thoughts pure and his body well and strong.

With the coming of the Sons of God to this planet to incarnate, there were added to the band of colors already surrounding it two higher cosmic currents or colors. The first three, the orange, the red, and the green, were all that were needed to ensoul the earth and the vegetable and animal kingdoms. But when the Sons of God came here to dwell, being of a higher rate of vibration than any thing on earth, their evolution depended upon the presence of higher forces from which they could draw. Having been created out of those portions of the Universal Consciousness which vibrate as blue and yellow their mental sup-' plies had to be drawn from the cosmic currents out of which they had been created. For man is the connecting link between the Celestial Beings of other Cosmic Days and the lower creatures of his own day, and it is through him and his efforts that the lower kingdoms will be raised to a higher development. Without the blue and the yellow cosmic currents he could not continue to maintain his present position in the Universe, but would deteriorate into the same general rate of vibration as the creatures below him that draw their support from the lower cosmic currents.

With these conditions in view the prudent psychic begins to lay the foundation for future clairvoyancy or Seership by getting his body into the proper condition in a scientific manner; for he knows that without a sound body and a wholesome mind his psychic development would be more harmful than helpful. Independent clairvoyance and clairaudience belong to man's mental and spiritual development and come only by consciously using the cosmic currents blue and yellow. Instructions how to gain these attributes of soul will be given in Lecture Five; at present physical and psychic development will be discussed, since these two things are the basis or foundation for the higher attributes to rest upon.

The first races of mankind that existed upon the

earth were powerful in their physique; "there were giants in those days;" and at that time men were supplied with several physical organs which have now either disappeared entirely or have diminished in size to infinitesimal and apparently useless glands. The diminution of these organs was caused by the sexual excesses which man indulged in and to the artificial modes of living which he adopted. For example, the tiny gland in the center of his brain which medical science calls the pineal gland was once a center of consciousness used by men for the purpose of functioning upon the psychic plane.[1] It was the organ through which the ego reported psychic events to the material plane. At the end of his auditory nerves there were other glands or centers of consciousness which the soul used to transmit psychic vibrations into audible sounds. But because he grew to love the material things of earth more than the psychic or mental, he neglected and finally ceased to use those centers of consciousness. With the disuse of an organ it diminishes in size and strength and after long continued disuse it becomes atrophied, and so it was with these centers in man's brain. Because of his grossness and sexual excesses, and the selfish and brutal conditions into which man sank, his psychic centers dwindled to glands very little larger than pin heads and became of no use whatever to him.

The same condition became true of other organs in his body. Originally there was an extra receptacle

---

[1]The History and Power of Mind, p. 184.

attached to the cæcum or head of the intestinal colon, now called the vermiform appendix, which served the purpose of retaining a vital fluid abstracted from food during the process of digestion, and which supplied sufficient nutriment to enable them to exist for weeks and sometimes for months without taking any other food. Now the miserable remnant of that once wonderful organ has degenerated into a cause of much suffering for mankind in general, and a source of considerable revenue for some of the members of the medical profession, who, while proceeding to remove the now useless attachment, wonder for what purpose it was ever created.

Ancient man was also supplied with a pair of glands, situated just above his kidneys, which medical science now calls suprarenal bodies. These bodies were created for the purpose of secreting other precious fluids vitally necessary to the prolongation of his physical life; but like the psychic centers in his brain these organs have also become obsolete, and all because of the neglect and abuse of his physical body.

At the present time in the cycle of evolution, during the last half of the sixth great period of our Cosmic Day, man is beginning to bestir himself, and is trying to regain some of the powers he once possessed and wasted so extravagantly. It is encouraging to note that the rising generations have begun to depart from the customs of the generations passing and are devoting more time to athletics. Twenty or thirty years ago it was considered quite the proper thing for wealthy men's sons to be effeminate fops. The heaviest things the fashionable scions of some of the old aristocratic families lifted or attempted to carry were their fancy-headed canes, which they sat and sucked while they idly stared out of their clubhouse windows at the women who passed. They did nothing and knew nothing outside the regular routine of the useless, indolent lives they lived. And the most arduous things the young women of that class and generation did was to practice a little piano music and eat bon bons. Both sexes were pale and puny and usually died quite young. Physical degeneracy reached its ultimate at that period. But the rising generation seems to have caught step with the law of evolution and is cultivating its physical strength. And although it may not realize what great benefit will be derived from so doing, yet is surely laying the foundation for a magnificent physique for the coming race.

As it has always been with every new impulse in the right direction, there are persons who adopt an extreme view of everything and overdo whatever they undertake. By reason of their enthusiasm in believing that if a little of a thing is good, a great deal is better, they are strongly inclined to excess in their atheletic exercises. To acquire health and strength it is not necessary or advisable to spring out of a warm bed in the morning and while the stomach is empty take a plunge into a tub of cold water; and then in order to bring the blood back to the surface of the body, from the vitals where it has been driven by the sudden shock, rub the skin until it smarts with the violent friction. But it is necessary to rise, bathe in tepid or warm water and dress deliberately and then open a window which lets the sunlight into the room, and while raising the arms to the highest point above the head, slowly fill the lungs to their greatest capacity with the pure oxygen of the morning. Then, as the breath is slowly exhaled, allow the arms to fall to the sides, and while this exercise is being repeated the thoughts should be concentrated upon the blue or yellow cosmic currents which surround the earth and supply man with his mental and spiritual forces.

It is not necessary to practice lifting great weights in order to strengthen the muscles and gain physical strength. Neither is it necessary to hang suspended by the heels in mid-air over a horizontal bar until the veins and arteries are ready to burst with the blood that is thus unnaturally forced into them. Man's Creators never intended that he should walk or stand upon his hands with his feet elevated in the air. An intelligent examination of his venous system will show that he was intended to walk or stand upon his feet and to use his hands and arms for other purposes than for walking. And such extreme exercises as these are not permanently helpful. For a time a man may feel thrills of exhilaration passing through his body because of his cold bath or of his exciting acrobatic performances, but there always comes a reaction from such shocks to his physical body the same as follows the drinking of a stimulant. The extra strength is not his to keep, but is borrowed from the future and will leave him as suddenly as it came.

Because it has been reported that an ancient hero practiced lifting a calf each day until it reached maturity and in this manner gained the strength to carry it when it became full grown, many of our modern heroes and athletes, who live where calves are not available, substitute iron dumb bells for infant bovines, and increase the weight of those bells until they sometimes strain themselves permanently. They forget—if they ever knew—that the strength they are now beginning to regain was lost ages and ages ago and that since it went gradually it will return gradually if they exercise in a wise and prudent manner.

Very few recognized athletes live to the age of fifty years and many die after about ten years of hard training. They suddenly collapse or go out with pneumonia or heart failure and people wonder why such strong men were unable to resist a severe cold when they could lift much more than their own weight. The reason is this: They had been overstraining their lungs and their muscles, and when the reaction came and they were placed upon a bed of illness their overstrained organs collapsed like an overcharged balloon.

Gentle, healthy exercises are both beneficial and necessary for man's physical and psychic development; but physical exercises should always be regulated by good judgment and common sense the same as should anything else that man does.

For an aid to the practice of concentration there are muscular exercises which are most beneficial and which serve to develop both the muscles and the mind. Instead of lifting heavy weights, it is a better exercise to concentrate the thoughts upon a particular muscle and learn to raise and lower it by the power of thought. The circulation of the blood in the body can also be controlled in like manner, and this is a better exercise than that of walking or of running for many miles. If a person desires to test the truth of this statement, let him concentrate his thoughts upon the blood in his feet. For five consecutive minutes let him think of nothing but his feet and the blood which is flowing into their veins and arteries. By seeing the veins throbbing and filled with blood in any portion of his body he will soon be able to control his circulation and strengthen and enlarge his muscles by his power of concentration.

If a person desires to enlarge and magnetize his brain and the psychic centers within it, let him concentrate his thoughts upon the tiny glands which are his physical and psychic centers of consciousness. Let him see the blue cosmic current flowing into those centres until they throb with this animating, magnetic fluid. But when his brain seems to be entirely filled with the current, and he feels it vibrating strongly, it is unwise to continue longer to draw upon it at that time. He should remember not to be any more extravagant in this than in any other exercise; for in the beginning of this practice he can overdo with his mental gymnastics the same as with physical athletics. In other words, he should be gentle and prudent with this as with every other thing he undertakes to do and not waste his precious force in tearing his body to pieces. It is much easier to destroy a thing than to construct it, and it requires much less time. There are mental as well as physical reactions, and it is well to avoid both as much as possible.

Now that man has reached the age of wireless telegraphy, it is not so difficult for him to understand how subjective sounds can be transmitted to the material plane. After witnessing the process of receiving from a ship in mid-ocean a message, and having it telephoned from the receiving station to his home, he can understand how the mind can transmit through its highly developed and sensitive instrument its message to the material world. But it is with this as with every other thing in the world that is done well, the proper conditions must exist in order to produce good results. If the receiving instrument is out of order the message will either not be received, or it will be imperfect and incomplete, and therefore will not be understood.

If the psychic's brain is befogged with the fumes of liquor or tobacco, or if the vibrations of his receiving glands and auditory nerves are deadened or stupefied by drugs or poisonous medicines he will not make a good transmitter of the message sent by the mind.

Therefore it is absolutely necessary that a good psychic should possess a good body. He must be sound in mind and body if he is to become an independent clairvoyant or clairaudient.

The imprudent manner in which psychic power has been manifested, is the chief cause of the disrepute from which psychism suffers at the present time. No thinking, intelligent person is apt to accept as true a thing that is told him by a wild-eyed, long-haired, pallid-faced person who poses before the public as a psychic. The woman who goes about the streets with her eyes half closed, whispering, muttering or gesticulating, is of no credit to the subject she is studying and is trying to present to the world.

The woman who tells everybody she knows and everybody she meets that she "is so psychic," or that she "examines psychically everything and everybody" she sees, is an unfortunate, misguided specimen of imprudent psychic development; for she has not a sound mind for the foundation of her development and is therefore totally unreliable in her statements. The prudently developed psychic will not dress differently nor appear conspicuous, but will always use his powers wisely. He will not advertise himself in any way as a psychic, nor will he seek notoriety. If he shares with a friend the knowledge he has gained he does so because he believes it will be of benefit to his friend, and not because he hopes or expects that in some way the giving will accrue to his own advantage.

There are many ways by which a lower order of psychic development can be gained, but two of the principal ones are through the Oriental method of breathing and yoga practices, and through the so-called spiritualistic developing circles of some of the Western students. Both methods usually produce a low order of mediumship which is never approved by the true Occultist.[1] For if Occultism stands for anything it is for the independent development of each individual ego, and not for the dependence of one ego upon another, whether incarnated or excarnated.

The material plane upon which man lives is interpenetrated by the first subjective plane which is crowded with disembodied entities who cannot get away from the material stage whereon they acted their various parts in the drama of life. It is perfectly natural that their dispositions and desires should not be changed by the laying down of their bodies. And it is natural that if they can find embodied egos whom they can influence or control they should try to do so, because it is the natural tendency of undeveloped natures to desire to manage other persons' affairs for them. There are hundreds of men and women in physical life who are ready to give advice to others about the most delicate and intricate matters pertaining to their private affairs and then bitterly resent it if their advice is not followed. And it is the same kind of egos upon the first psychic plane who offer themselves as "heavenly guides" to mortals.

[1]The History and Power of Mind, pp. 168-184.

The disembodied entity who succeeds in gaining sufficient influence over a psychic to control in any way his thoughts or actions, commences to draw upon the magnetism of that person from the first moment the attachment between them is formed. And if its influence is permitted to continue, if the psychic is quite willing and anxious to be led by his "heavenly guide," there will soon be additions made to his "group of controls" and this will continue until he becomes possessed by a whole "band" and never for a moment will he be acting independently or according to his own judgment. He is never permitted to think for himself, but is constantly impressed with the thoughts of others who do his thinking for him, and while they give to him their often mistaken ideas, they draw from him his physical magnetism until he becomes a nervous wreck. He becomes their magnetic dynamo or supply station from which they take copiously.

He permits his business—if he has any—to be conducted under the guidance of an entity who was an Indian warrior and whose business during his last earthly experience was that of hunting and fishing and taking scalps. If the psychic fails in business he wonders what was the cause of his failure, since he followed faithfully the directions of his "Indian guide."

In his marital relationship he may be guided by an entity who in earth life was a polygamist, and who still believes in a plurality of wives. If the psychic

finds himself incarcerated in prison for the crime big-
amy while acting under the guidance of this "control." he wonders how it could have happened.   Further explanation of the psychic plane and its relation
to the physical world is given in Lecture Ten.

Yoga practices for psychic development are older
than the written history of mankind and were used
by the priests on the Continent Atlantis, which is
now sunken beneath the sea.   The yoga of to-day has
degenerated from its original purpose of upbuilding
the body and brain of man and has become a dangerous and most degenerate practice.   The Occultists say
it was used by the first teachers of the races, by the
Avatars and the Saviours, for the purpose of raising
man's mind from the material things of earth to the
spiritual planes of thought; to produce perfect mental harmony between God and man.   In those ancient
days the priests and high priests retired into their
sanctuaries when they wished to commune with
Divine Mind, and, through meditation and concentration upon the Great Consciousness and the Celestial
Beings, received the spiritual enlightenment they
demanded.   But they did not indulge in the foolish
chastisement or scourging of their physical bodies as
do the yogi of the present day.   They did not sit upon
the ground in a single spot without moving until the
roots of a tree grew over their limbs. Neither did they
clench their hands and hold them in that position
until their nails grew into their palms.

There are Orientalists who teach Western students

the damaging and dangerous yoga breathing, for the purpose of stimulating or awakening psychic centers of consciousness in the body and the brain. The Occultist would warn against the practice. To many who read these lectures this warning will be unnecessary because their own limited experiences have brought about physical disturbances. These results are inevitable because the unnatural method of breathing suddenly changes the polarity of the brain and reverses the natural circulation of the blood, bringing abnormal pressure upon the Psychic centers in the brain. Because the brain controls the nerves of the body the entire nervous system is thus sympathetically affected. The sudden change from the natural to the unnatural manner of breathing renders the physical body negative and unable to resist an attack of epilepsy or obsession. The minor physical results manifest in one or more of the following forms: temporary blindness in one or both eyes, bleeding at the ears or nose, stammering and hysteria. If a person desires to know something further of the results of yoga breathings let him make a study of those who practice them, whether they are from the Orient or from the Occident. It is not difficult to find victims of this wretched practice in many of the insane asylums of this country and it is not possible to find one person who has gained anything in spiritual development by aid of them.

Swami Vive Kânanda, who introduced yoga breathing in this country, died, it is said, from the results

of his own practices. His demise was a great loss
to the world, however, for he was not only an able
man, but also a helper of humanity, and the Occident should revere his memory because he brought to
popular attention the beautiful Vedanta Philosophy.
His teacher, who suffered from epilepsy, died, it is
said, in an epileptic paroxysm caused by yoga practices. Many of the lesser lights in this line of work are
Americans who have adopted yoga breathing and
have attempted for a while to teach it, but since they
were not trained in it from childhood, the natural
consequences of a disarranged body and mind more
quickly followed their mistakes and they have disappeared very soon from public view as teachers,
leaving many wrecked lives behind them.

LECTURE FIVE.

MENTAL AND SPIRITUAL DEVELOPMENT.

"And the earth (Universe) was without form, and void (motionless); and darkness was upon the face of the deep."

Before any thing was made, God—Divine Mind—existed. It was and is and forever will be, Divine Potentiality; and it is also the Essence and the Substance of subjective and of objective things. It is of the Universe, and it is the Universe. It has no source, but it is the Source; and never having been born, It can never die. As Essence It is ineffable; but as Substance It is expressible.

"And the Spirit of God (Divine Mind) moved upon the face of the waters * * * and there was light."

As Divine Essence, It could only be Essential Perfection and Omnipresence. But as Divine Substance, It became substantial first as light. In Its nature It is fluidic and vibratory. In expression It became differentiated and diversified. As Omniscience It is Being: as Creative Gods, It became Beings. As God It is Mind; as men It became minds. As the Father-Mother, It is Consciousness. In man It became intuition; in the animal It became instinct, and in the plant It was and is consciousness.

Evolution, with its various and variable modes of expression, is the machinery that moves the Universe, and will, in its various aspects, is the propelling force that moves evolution. With the Celestial, Creative Beings, this force manifests as Divine Will. With man it becomes differentiated into two aspects. In the subjective mind it becomes individual will, while in man's objective mind it becomes individual desire. With animals. this force manifests as animal desire, and with all kinds of plant life it manifests as sub-conscious desire.

With its sub-conscious desire for greater freedom, better protection and more warmth, the tiny life germ in the heart of a seed bursts its confining limitations and sends forth, into the magnetic, mineralized soil below it, the fibrous roots that will serve as a conduit for the elements it sub-consciously needs. And as the tiny roots reach farther and deeper into the warm, damp soil, the dependent little seed seems to nestle closer and closer into the earth's maternal bosom, until it is completely covered. And there it receives the warmth and protection it sub-consciously desires. And when these demands have been freely and fully met, then it is the same sub-conscious desire —this time for greater freedom—that causes it to send into the atmosphere above the soil another means by which its further needs may be supplied. This time the means are not the cylindrical, porous roots that may serve only as tubes through which moisture and fertilized nutrition shall be drawn, but it is something not unlike a tiny sail, and is an emblem of its coming freedom.

The sail is tightly furled when it first appears and thus it remains until it begins to feel the sun's light and heat, and then, sub-consciously, it gradually unfurls and, like a cup, it holds itself in readiness to receive the rain-drops and the dew, as well as all the sunshine it can get; for these things are as necessary to its maintenance as are the chemicals it draws from out the soil. And when it has reached a point in its development where it must fulfil its parental mission, that same sub-conscious desire which first caused it to become established as a plant puts forth the tiny buds and blossoms and then the fruit, which bears within its heart the seed for more sub-consciousness to ensoul. By reason of its accumulated strength, gained from maintaining individualized form for many years, out of sub-consciousness, consciousness is born. And since desire can only be where consciousness exists, and since desire becomes intensified as consciousness gains strength, sub-conscious desire becomes desire, and through its propelling force, brings sub-consciousness into expression in greater and still higher forms of consciousness.[1]

It was the sub-conscious desire for better protection and more warmth that caused the life germ in the seed to reach down into the soil, and it was the same sub-conscious desire for greater freedom which caused it to send its green cups above the soil and into

---

[1] The History and Power of Mind, pp. 69-71.

the sunlight. As its sub-conscious desire grew, still greater freedom was its constant demand, until, after many years of limitation as a plant, the time came when it was strong enough to be born into a higher form, and thus it came into a realization of its sub-conscious demand for greater freedom.

In insect life sub-consciousness becomes a lower form of consciousness and ensouls whole swarms of tiny forms. For example, the sub-consciousness of a decaying shrub will be sufficient to ensoul a thousand ants that will work and build their hills while controlled by the conscious desire of the swarm. Each ant depends upon the swarm consciousness and upon itself to do its part of the whole, and in this new form receives the freedom it desired as a shrub; and thus the ant or lower state of consciousness is born. In the higher form as animal, the lower consciousness of the swarm has given way and, out of it, independent animal desire is born. Its consciousness has grown in strength until now it may be called a mind, because it thinks independently and has a voice and can express its thoughts in acts as well as sounds. It also has a greater freedom than it had as a swarm of ants, for with its growth desire has also grown, and where once its needs were few they now have multiplied to many. Where once it stood a shrub, content to be alone, it now demands companions and possessions. Like the swarm of ants, it desires an abiding place, but now it also wants a mate. It loves and hates and desires to rule its kind. Conscious of itself, it desires to provide for self regardless of the wants or needs of others: and here another quality appears. Instinct is born of individual consciousness with animal desire for its sire, and instinct helps to improve and preserve the animal form and to continue its existence until it reaches man's estate.

And when the objective mind or animal soul has become endowed with the subjective mind or immortal soul, it is at this point in the evolution of the lower mind that conscience appears to do its work. At first it seems to be not larger, nor stronger, nor of more importance than the tiny glow worm, which is sometimes seen among the weeds and grasses, on a summer evening. And like the glow worm, conscience at first can only flash a faint light into the darkness of man's animal soul, and then only for a moment does it attract, for it cannot hold his attention. But when it has become enthroned in the animal man's soul it continues to flash and flame its immortal light upon his every thought and act. With every advantage gained it gains in strength until it becomes to him not only a light but a "still small voice," which, though so faint and weak at first that it can but whisper, yet in the innermost chamber of his mind it tells him truths which his dearest friend or boldest enemy dare not tell. It never pays him false compliments nor seeks to palliate his sins with soft and gentle words. It calls his vices by their proper names and shows him mental pictures of the crimes he has committed.

Many persons believe that conscience is the voice of God speaking to man, directing his actions and reproving his mistakes. And many believe that if he becomes conscienceless he has "grieved the Spirit," and It has left him; or in the language of the Church, he has "sinned away his day of grace." There are others who believe that conscience is mind and think that it manifests in domestic animals, and especially in their own particular pets. If conscience were mind alone it would be possessed by wild beasts as well as by domesticated creatures, for mind, or the power to think, is not confined exclusively to animals that have been blest by their association with man.

The occultist would say that the faculty which seems to resemble conscience in the animal is instinct, which is really the mother of conscience. The animal has a memory of its past mistakes and their consequent punishments, and remembers the pain it suffered in connection with the acts which produced the pain; and it is the desire for self-preservation and the fear of a repetition of suffering which prevents it from repeating again and again the same mistakes. But conscience is born of animal instinct with a Son of God for its sire. It is the mental product or mental result of the association of an animal mind and its instinct with its subjective mind, and is to that mind what thought is to both minds. It is a tool, an instrument which the subjective mind uses in its work of conquering and educating its lower mind.

An infant conscience, like any other infant, is born

very weak and small, and in the beginning sleeps much of its time. But after being fed upon the nutritious food of experience, which it draws through its mother instinct, it gradually grows larger and stronger, and where, to the undeveloped man, it whispers so faintly that he sometimes does not hear its words above the din and furor he is making, to the advanced man, to him who has consciously claimed his Divine Heritage, it speaks in thunderous tones.

With many persons the emotion sympathy is often mistaken for conscience, and because of this mistake many times man's reason and judgment are swept aside, and, while he believes he is following the dictates of his conscience, he is really permitting his emotions to direct his actions. Like passion, sympathy is a tremendous force, and if it be not controlled by wisdom, and if it is permitted to have full sway, it often causes men to make mistakes the results of which will require many lives of suffering to correct.

It is sympathy and not conscience which creates the sentiment that causes war and raises armies of men for the purpose of fighting with such of their fellows as do not agree with them in principle. It was sympathy for the Southern slave which created the unconscientious sentiment that brought the men of the Northern and Southern portions of the United States into battle. And when those battles were at their height it was another emotion, called patriotism, which caused the men of one nation—brothers of one family—to commit crimes against each other, which, under normal mental conditions, they would never have done. During the din and excitement of battle the voice of conscience is never heard; but when the confusion is ended and the wounded or dying soldier lies upon the battlefield alone with God, he then has time to listen to his conscience, which says:

"After all, there is no real satisfaction in knowing that you have killed other men, who, perhaps, had wives and children who loved them as dearly as yours love you. You are not a hero, but in God's sight, because you have taken lives which you cannot restore and which are as precious to Him as is your own, you are a murderer. And some time you will be brought face to face with the souls you have so recklessly and needlessly sent out of life."

The men who rush to hang the trembling wretch, who, in a moment of uncontrolled animal passion, has outraged a member of their community, are not actuated by their consciences to commit a crime as great as that of the man they are seeking to punish. For, like the frightened wretch they wish to kill, they, too, are controlled by their emotions, and the only difference between the actuating causes of the two crimes is the difference in sentiment which controls the perpetrators. The first crime was caused by the emotion called sexual passion, and the last one was caused by the passion called anger, which had its birth in sympathy for the outraged member of their community. Anger and sexual passion both belong to the lowest, darkest shade of the red cosmic current, into which the punished and the punishers had fallen. But after the victim of the mob's passion had paid with his life the penalty the mob demanded, and when the men who sent him out of physical life had time to listen to their consciences, each man found the picture of his victim photographed upon his mind, and it mattered not which way he turned to avoid it, that awful sight turned with him. If he awoke suddenly in the night, it was there, and he had to see it in all its dreadful details. It arose between him and the faces of his dear ones, and even at the moment when he was boastfully telling of the manner in which he helped to rid the country of an outlaw, his conscience was saying: "You know you are as great a criminal as the man you helped to kill."

It is not conscience which actuates the sheriff to adjust the rope around the neck of a murderer and then step upon the spring which unlocks the trap beneath the feet of his victim. His objective mind may temporarily convince him that his act is a noble one, and that he is really a public benefactor. But when he has entered into his closet and has shut the door between himself and the outside world; when all the excitement and publicity has passed, then it is the voice of conscience which says to him:

"You are a murderer, too, and have committed as great a crime as that of the man you killed. The emotion which actuated his sin was anger, while yours was greed. He killed the man who he believed had wronged him, while you killed him because you were hired to do it by the State. You are a hired assassin and are no better than the highwayman who shoots and kills his victim for the money he may have in his pocket. You strangled this man for the paltry sum the State offered to you for doing its bloody work." And then one of two things will occur: Either the sheriff will resign his position as public executioner and go into a better business or he will refuse to listen to his conscience and will continue to kill the men whom the State orders him to kill. If he chooses the latter then the voice of his conscience will gradually grow fainter and weaker until it will finally become silent, and as a consequence the animal nature of that man will grow morally worse and sink lower and lower into brutality until it becomes so gross that its subjective mind will be obliged to abandon it to its fate; for a conscienceless man is indeed a lost animal soul, and, without the enlightening power of its subjective mind, will continue in the downward path to ultimate destruction.

Some one may ask: "If conscience is what the Occultist says it is; if every individual conscience is the offspring of a Son of God, why are not all consciences alike? Why is not the conscience of a black cannibal in the wilds of Africa as reproving as the conscience of a Tolstoi or of a Gladstone?"

The Occultist would say that the black cannibal belongs to the last race of animal men in which the Sons of God incarnated upon earth, and the animal natures of the last races were so strong that they ruled their higher or subjective minds through many reincarnations. And it was not until those higher minds had suffered the painful consequences of obeying the dictations of their lower minds that they learned to struggle for the supremacy. The subjective mind of a Gladstone or a Tolstoi has had many more experiences than has that of the black cannibal, because it came to earth among the first group of incarnating egos while the black man was among the last of the subjective minds or souls who came. The mind who wore the personality of a Tolstoi or of a Gladstone has reincarnated more times than has the mind of the cannibal. Because of its mistakes the advanced ego has seen continents sink beneath the sea, and because of its ignorance and wrong doing it has been swept out of material life again and again by earthquakes and by cataclysms. It has also suffered torture at the hands of its fellowmen until it has learned to command instead of obey its own lower mind. Where once it whispered to its animal nature through the voice of an infant conscience, it now speaks in the commanding tone of a conscious soul, and as a Tolstoi or a Gladstone its reproofs are listened to by other objective minds as well as by its own.

Acting under the dictates of its conscience, mankind has evolved to a condition where it begins to understand life's problems from a higher mental plane than that of the animal mind; and, as man's objective mind becomes subservient to his subjective mind, the animal instinct merges into intuition, and animal desire becomes absorbed by individual will. At this point, man, conscious of his heritage as a Son of God, begins to claim some of his powers and privileges. In religion he has begun to claim his divine right to think for himself and to worship as suits him best. And instead of continuing under the dominion of the Church and under the direction of its so-called holy men, he decides to accept only such truths as appeal to him as truths. Sometimes he stands forth among his fellowmen as a moralist and refuses to recognize the need of either church or religious society to help him to keep in the path of rectitude. And he declares that he will live according to the light of conscience, and not according to the man-made creeds and dogmas of the Church, and it is at this point in his evolution, if he makes the most of his opportunities, that he will become fitted for a higher spiritual life, for this is the intermediate stage between the animal and spiritual man.

When old institutions are forced to give way to new, there are always many things said and done on both sides which are to be regretted. When the men and women who felt that they could no longer conscientiously indorse or subscribe to the creeds of the Church, and for that reason stepped outside that ancient and crumbling institution, they, and the ethical societies which they formed, were anathematized by their former religious associates. When first they boldly declared themselves to be doers of good for the sake of good, and not for Jesus' sake or for the sake of future heavenly rewards, or because of the fear of future punishment, many of their religious friends declared that all their ethical societies were but cesspools of iniquity, and that they, themselves, were infidels. Many names, from among this class of courageous souls, were dropped from the visiting lists of those who still continued to worship an anthropomorphic God and to fear a cloven-footed devil. Some of the more kindly disposed of the church people felt that it was necessary to go in search of the lost sheep, and many made it a religious duty to call upon and "labor with" those early seceders, spending much time and some patience in their efforts to bring back to the fold of the Church the wandering few.[1] But returning to the Church after having tasted the freedom of thought and the freedom of speech that are accorded to the independent moralist would be like half-grown birds returning to the nest where they were hatched. It was an impossible thing to accomplish, and proved to be labor lost for the anxious ones who undertook the task. But what seemed to the Church to be a sad misfortune really proved to be a blessing in disguise, because, after a time, the liberality of thought and speech of its ex-members began to have a broadening effect upon such of their Church friends as would listen to their views. And the result was that many of the creeds and dogmas of the

---

[1]Mata the Magician, pp. 176-182.

Church have been revised and many of the objectionable and unreasonable tenets have been eliminated.

No longer does the congregation of the modern Church hear of infant damnation, and the Calvinistic theory of fore-ordination is now never touched upon in the pulpit by any of the modern clergymen. This great change and improvement has been brought about by the advanced thought expressed by the independent moralist, the members of the ethical societies, the Mental and Christian Scientists, and the advanced thinkers who refuse to wear the label of any "ism" or "ist." This has indeed become the "Age of Reason," which Thomas Paine foresaw and wrote about so many years ago; and it is also the age of mental power for the progressive man, who now begins to realize the fact that he must become the master of his mind before he can reach the spiritual plane of thought. He finds that his physical and mental environment must be controlled before he can enter into the realm of spirit.

On his way toward spirituality man finds many avenues which, since he has become an independent thinker, seem necessary to explore. If while in his undeveloped state he had become a psychic, and was conscious of the faces and of the forms of earth-bound entities who could not get away from the material plane, he may now, with his knowledge and power of mind, become clairvoyant and see the planes of being and the souls who have passed beyond the earth. And where once he only heard the confused murmurings of the psychic plane nearest the earth, he may now, with his increased power, become clairaudient and listen to the music of the spheres.

The Century Dictionary defines clairvoyance as a power attributed to persons in a mesmeric state by which they are supposed to discern objects concealed from sight, and to see what is happening at a distance. It also defines clairaudience as the supposed power of hearing, in a mesmeric trance, sounds which are not audible to the ear in a waking state. Both of these definitions are confusing because each makes the clairvoyant and clairaudient condition depend upon the subject being in a mesmeric state—which statement is untrue. The individual who is dependent upon being mesmerized by another, in order to function upon any subjective plane, is neither a clairvoyant nor a clairaudient. He is simply a psychic and his statements are not to be relied upon, because while under the influence of another, his mind is under the mental control of another mind and his vision is likely to be imperfect and to be colored by the thoughts and perhaps by the mistaken beliefs of the mesmerist. He sees, as it were, through another's spectacles, which perhaps are not at all fitted to his eyes. He also may hear or think he hears what the mesmerist hopes, wishes or believes he will hear.

But the independent clairvoyant is one who has purified his life and has raised the vibrations of his body and brain to a point where his material vehicle is no longer a veil for mind, and therefore he is no longer blinded by it. In order to develop or improve his clairvoyant vision he takes the time, during his devotional hours, to draw from the cosmic currents surrounding the earth the forces which were placed there solely for his benefit, and which will increase the rate of vibration of his brain and of also the psychic centres within it. Commencing with the cosmic blue he concentrates upon it until it is drawn like a cloud about him, and while he rests and bathes in this great force he watches the psychic centres in his brain as they vibrate higher and stronger under its vivifying power. Commencing with the shade of cosmic blue which he can use most easily, through concentration, he gradually raises the shade to higher and higher rates until it fades into the next higher color, the yellow. And then he draws the golden yellow to himself and basks in its uplifting spiritual light until his brain has had all that it can bear and demands a rest. Then the wise individual will sleep for a few moments, and when he wakes again he will be greatly strengthened and uplifted both in body and mind, and he will also find that in time his clairvoyant vision is cleared and strengthened by the experience.

He is now at a point in his development where he may demand to be omniscient and omnipotent; and when his demands are answered and the spiritual forces come sweeping through him from the higher planes of being, for a little time, he may become unconscious of the trials and sorrows of physical life and in the great Beyond commune with egos who have preceded him on their evolutionary journey. If he is sufficiently purified he may be able to see or to visit the third or even the fourth plane of spiritual consciousness while his physical body rests quietly awaiting his return. And he may be permitted to participate for a few hours in the happiness of some of the egos who dwell in that beautiful place.

Happiness is attained through spiritual growth and is not the result of a gratification of the desires for material things; and spirituality, in its different degrees, is gained only through becoming positively good and positively pure. It is the glory surrounding wisdom as sunlight is the glory surrounding the sun, and is never the result of negativeness or of ignorance.

On this material plane it is often said of a slender, pale-faced, negatively good woman, "she is spiritual." But a careful interview with the so-called spiritual person, discloses the fact that her spirituality is but a potentiality which will require many lives filled with trying and perhaps bitter experiences to actualize. It is to the confounding of the word spirit with ghost that this mistake is largely due. Since the story of the Witch of Endor was written, mankind has believed that all ghosts are spirits and that an ego becomes a spirit as soon as its material body is laid aside. It is by mistaken analogy that men have founded this belief concerning persons. Because a ghost is supposed to be tall, slender and white, it has become a general belief that height and pallor and a willowy form are spiritual requisites, and that without them it is impossible to be or to become spiritual. Knowing this to be a race belief, many persons of both sexes who are possessed of these indications of physical imperfections use them with the credulous public to trade upon.

The tall, cadaverous clergyman who rises to his full height of six feet in the pulpit, and waves his long, thin arms above his head while he solemnly denounces sin and sinners, often awakens more reverence in the hearts of the people of his congregation than does the short, stout, rosy-faced man whose head and shoulders just appear above the desk while he teaches that men should not do unto others what they would not have others to do unto them. Forty-nine persons out of every fifty who help to compose the congregation of the cadaverous clergyman declare him to be a "spiritual man," notwithstanding his bitterness and vituperous denunciations, and not one ever thinks of attributing spirituality to the pleasant-faced, smiling little pastor who tries to teach them a basic principle of life. Yet in point of fact he is a long step further on in his development than the other one, and is much nearer to gaining spirituality, because he has love in his heart while the other has vindictiveness in his heart and ecclesiastical doctrines and creeds in his head.

And among the members of churches and religious societies there are also many persons whose stock in trade is their pallor and their long, bony bodies. They pose before the world as "spiritual," because of their resemblance to ghosts, and, if they lecture, or heal, or teach, or if they are psychics they too command a reverence and respect for a spirituality which they do not possess or know nothing of as yet. Many women who are negatively good because they have not been tempted, or who have not had an opportunity in this life to go wrong, are called "spiritual" by those who do not know that only an ego is spiritual who has gained wisdom by overcoming its animal nature. According to the Occultists a spiritual person is one whose intuition has become awakened, and whose will has absorbed its desire; one who has become purified through suffering and who is good because he loves goodness more than anything else in the Universe; one who tells the truth because it is true; and is pure because he loves purity and not because he fears a present or a future punishment.

To the clairvoyant vision of such a one the spiritual planes of being are opened and it receives what it has earned for its labors. It has fought its way back to its divine heritage, and, as a returned prodigal Son of God, receives its share of Omniscience and Omnipotence.

Between the spiritual and material planes is the mental plane, and it is as impossible for man to become spiritual before his mental powers are developed as it is for a dog to speak English. The intelligent dog may know that there is such a thing as language, and he may be able to understand the few words which he is most accustomed to hear spoken, but he has not the power of speech nor will he gain that power, until he has evolved to the point where he can become enlightened by a subjective mind of his own. It is true that his development may be hastened by his association with men, and that through an intelligent method of training he may gain much more rapidly than he would if left to evolve by himself. But he will never speak a word until he becomes a human being, and it would be folly to expect him to. And in a like manner it is impossible for animal man to become spiritual man until his mental powers have been developed to a point which makes him receptive to spiritual things.

Spirituality is composed of three attributes, Omniscience, Omnipotence and Omnipresence, and unless an ego has acquired, to a greater or lesser degree, something of the first two he cannot claim to be a spiritual soul. The first attribute of spirituality to be gained is Omniscience, which means to have gained all knowledge. An ego must know how to act before it can act wisely: and in order to gain and possess something of this spiritual attribute, man's power of concentration must be increased until he can place his thoughts upon something beside himself and hold them there until he has mentally absorbed the knowledge he desired concerning that thing. How can a man be or become in any degree Omniscient, when his power of concentration is so weak that he cannot hold his thoughts for five consecutive minutes on a single subject?

Omnipotence is the next higher attribute of spirituality and means to have all power. To gain or possess Omnipotence, in any degree, man must at least be able to concentrate upon and use the spiritual cosmic forces blue and yellow, and he must have evolved to a point of development where he can demonstrate over disease and disharmony in his own mind and also, at least temporarily, remove it from the bodies and minds of others. He must possess enough Omnipotence to give him power over his own lower nature and power to control his own environment. And after he has gained this attribute in ever so small a degree he will never again become a victim of circumstances nor an object of charity.

Omnipresence means to be everywhere present at the same time, and this is the last aspect of spirituality. It also can be gained only through mental development and spiritual power. To become capable of being everywhere present a mind must be untrammelled by form and must become one with Divine Mind. It must have lost its desire for individuality and become absorbed by the Universal Principle. To the Western Occultist this aspect of spirituality is not a desirable ultimate to be attained, and, since greater and higher individualization is the goal to which he aspires, he never demands Omnipresence. To the students of the Eastern school of Occultism, however, to gain Nirvana and Omnipresence is to reach the highest condition of spiritual happiness that can be attained in the Universe; and some demand and receive it. This spiritual condition is very beautifully described in "The Light of Asia," in "Book the Eighth," where it says:

"No need hath such to live as ye name life;
  That which began in him when he began
Is finished; he hath wrought the purpose through
  Of what did make him man.

Never shall yearnings torture him, nor sins
  Stain him, nor ache of earthly joys and woes
Invade his safe eternal peace; nor death
  And lives recur. He goes

Unto Nirvana. He is one with Life
  Yet lives not. He is blest, ceasing to be.
Om, mani padme om! the dewdrop slips
  Into the shining sea!"

For the utterly tired soul who feels that to be reabsorbed and thus be able to rest forever in the bosom of the Infinite, without an individual care or responsibility, Omnipresence is the necessary spiritual attribute to demand in order to reach that state. But it is never well to make that demand until an ego has gained Omniscience, in order that it may know all things, and Omnipotence, in order that it may have all power, and thus be able to decide its fate without prejudice or passion.

LECTURE SIX.

FOCUSING FORCES.

Since at the present time the scientists of the world disagree as to the actual construction of the atom; and because they have never seen one, they are uncertain whether it is really the smallest division of matter, or whether it is a corpuscle composed of still smaller divisions, so as a preliminary explanation, and for the purpose of avoiding future controversy or criticism, the position of the Occultist will be defined before proceeding further.

In Occultism the word atom has always meant the smallest division of matter;[1] and so long as the English language continues to be spoken, the Occultist will call that infinitesimal division of substance by its original name. And it will make no difference how often the men of science advance beyond or recede from their present or future positions, or whether they call the atom an ion, a corpuscle, an electrical invisible or some other name, to the Occultist it is and ever will be an atom.

Everything, from the greatest and most sublime to the smallest and most insignificant center of consciousness, is generating and possesses powers which

[1]The History and Power of Mind, pp. 38-39; 41-42.

manifest, in its individual radius or sphere, as attraction and repulsion. And whether a center belongs to the constructive or destructive side of nature depends upon its mode of manifestation. If it manifests as attraction more than as repulsion then it is more constructive than destructive. If it manifests more as repulsion than as attraction then it is more destructive than constructive. To the working of the law of evolution, however, both manifestations are equally essential in order that progression may be constant and continuous, since it is absolutely necessary that old forms of expression should be destroyed to make room for new forms which will continue to exist after the old ones have ceased to serve the purposes for which they were created.

Before power either of constructive or destructive nature can be generated its center or basis of force must be formed; and, paradoxical as it may seem, it is nevertheless a truth that while the formation of a center is absolutely necessary to the generation of force, yet the generation of force is also the direct cause of the center it manifests through. The atom is an individual center of force; and, like all other centers, whether great or small, has two distinct motions, which are rotary and elliptical. And without these two motions it would be utterly impossible for God—Divine Mind—to be fully expressed in Its various and varied forms of manifestation. For the generation of power a center is dependent upon its rotary motion. But for the expression of manifestation of power, whether it be constructive or de-structive, it is dependent upon its elliptical motion. And both these motions are directly due to the vibra-tions which were eminated by Divine Will in the be-ginning of this Cosmic Day or period of evolution.

Vibration came into existence through the mental demand or command: "Let there be light." And vibration will continue until the last moment of this Cosmic Day, when God—Divine Mind—will desire rest. Then the demand or command, "Peace, be still," will go forth throughout the Universe, and gradually the vibratory and the rotary motion of the greatest centers of force in the heavens will begin to decrease; and as the vibration in them diminishes, their light will begin to fade. With a diminution of their constructive or rotary motion their elliptical motion will decrease and finally cease. And with the cessation of all motion or vibration there can no longer be a magnetic attraction between them and any other existing bodies or centers. Under these conditions the planets in the various systems will no longer continue to revolve around their respective centers or suns. They will no longer be attracted or repelled by each other, and each part composing the planet will no longer be attracted or repelled by other parts, and thus the manifested portion of the Universe will again become reduced to primordial substance.[1]

The coming of this great change is tersely described in Matthew, twenty-fourth chapter and twenty-ninth

---

[1] The History and Power of Mind, p. 100.

verse, where it is written: "In those days shall the sun be darkened, and the moon shall not give her light, and the stars shall fall (disappear) from heaven, and the powers of the heavens shall be shaken."

And since it is a law of the Supreme Consciousness to rest equally as long as it labors, the Cosmic Nights are of as great length as are the Cosmic Days, and thus for eons will the Universe be at rest without a ripple or a wave within that Sea of Unconsciousness, until the time shall come for another Cosmic Day to dawn; then the command will go forth again for light, and again will the greater and smaller centers of force be roused from their inactivity. "In the place where the tree falleth there it shall be," and in the place where a powerful center of force ceased to vibrate, there it remains in a fluidic, primordial condition, awaiting the Divine summons to start within it the vibratory force which will make it possible for it again to assume a form and to fulfill its mission in the Universe.[1]

As an illustration of the manner in which constructive and destructive forces are used in the formation and disintegration of worlds, a few pages will be quoted from the diary of an advanced student of Occultism, who, with his Master's assistance, was enabled to leave his physical body, and while thus liberated was permitted to study cosmogony from the standpoint of a temporarily disembodied soul.

---

[1]The History and Power of Mind, p. 102.

"When first I slipped from my body, as the letter slips from its envelope, I was conscious of standing beside my material vehicle and of looking down upon it as it lay helpless and apparently a corpse before me. At first I experienced a shock of surprise, and then a slight feeling of alarm; but upon looking closely I found that my body was still breathing faintly, and I also saw that the heart was beating slowly. Somewhat reassured, I turned toward my Master, who was waiting for me to accompany him into space. He, too, had liberated himself from his physical body and stood before me in all the glory of a Spiritual Being. And, as I gazed at Him in this new condition, for the first time since commencing my studies in Occultism, did I fully realize what soul freedom meant. Then, as He reached out a hand to me and said: 'come,' it seemed as if I were suddenly filled with a tremendous force, and at that moment I realized that I was tasting the glory of Omniscience and of Omnipotence. When I touched His hand I seemed to expand in size, and where once my aura had only extended for about a foot beyond the confining limitations of my rather undersized physical body, now, while holding to His hand, I seemed almost to fill the little room I called my den. Full of this new force, I rose like a balloon in midair, and for a few moments we remained suspended over the housetops of the city. And while we paused and looked downward, I saw the members of my family and many of my friends going about their duties, unconscious of the fact that roofs and walls were not able to hide them from the eyes of a Soul. This was my first spiritual object lesson, and I decided never again in the supposed privacy of my room to do anything which I would be ashamed to do in the presence of a friend.

"After this—to me—a very important decision was made, we rose to a distance of perhaps a thousand feet, and there we paused and again looked down upon the old world that was rolling so rapidly beneath us. As we journeyed I watched the towns and villages and cities of North America pass below us like a panorama; and finally I saw the Pacific Ocean and the Orient, and then my study in topography was suddenly interrupted by a change in our movements. I became conscious of whizzing through space with the speed of the wind. Looking downward, I saw the earth a diminishing ball, and it was apparently sinking away from me. We had entered another atmosphere; that of the earth, through which we had been passing, had disappeared. After a time we became surrounded by myriads of brilliant, scintillating particles which were whirling, floating, sweeping and eddying in all directions. That part of space seemed to be completely filled with that strange substance, and in answer to my mental question of what it was, I was impressed with the thought that this was what the scientists called 'cosmic dust.' It was formed into great clouds of vibrating atoms, which were plainly visible to the eye of soul, and which were being drawn into a common center.[1]

---

[1]The History and Power of Mind, p. 105.

"After passing through clouds of the billowy stuff we withdrew to a distance and watched the tremendous forces at work upon it. At a point in space, so far above us that it seemed to be very little larger than the world which we had left, was a brilliant spot in the heavens, and out of it were pouring great floods of what seemed to be ráys of electric light, and the focusing point for those rays was in the center of the mass of scintillating atoms before us. In response to my mental question regarding the nature of that wondrous center of light, my Master replied: 'That is a group of Elohim, sometimes called Planetary Spirits, and They are now focusing their forces upon this Their creation. As a group They generate the power which They send forth in those great constructive streams which look like electric light; and if you will carefully observe you will see that when those streams reach this point in space, the distance has been so well calculated that if they were not focused to form a center here, they would each form an elliptical circuit and return to the Center from which it emanated. But, meeting as they do at this point, a new center of force is formed, and because of the rapid vibrations of those particles of cosmic dust, and because of the rotary motion given to the entire mass, a vortex is formed, which, by its own generating power, will continue to draw to itself more and more of the detached floating atoms within its radius.'

"The scene before me was beautiful and wonderful, yet awful, for I was looking upon a throbbing, pulsating mass of brilliant substance. Above, below, beyond, as far as I could see, were mountainous heaps of that silvery, foamy mass. Sometimes it seemed like great clouds of steam with prismatic coloring thrown upon it by calcium lights, or it assumed the hue of smoke and curled and twisted like huge serpents in a fearful embrace. Suddenly there would stream forth from the heaving mass sharp, red, forked tongues of fire, which blazed fiercely for a time and then disappeared, to be replaced by banks of billowy cloud, while in deep diapason tones, first crescendo and then diminuendo, I heard something that sounded like the vibrating notes from innumerable organ pipes. Where the music came from I did not know, but it seemed to have been produced by the will of some great Master of harmony; and, as though the thought had been put into my mind, I realized that at this point was being generated a center of force which in the course of future ages would become a terrestrial globe, and this strange sound was the 'music of the spheres' that I had read about but had never heard before.

"Suddenly I became conscious of a sound like the hissing of steam, and the shrieking of the elements as though a great wind were blowing and a storm rising. In the distance I saw a blazing ball of fire coming toward us. Behind it was a brilliant train of fiery sparks; and as it approached I saw the flash of jagged lightning and heard the peal of thunder. My Master said: 'You are about to witness the grandest spectacle to be seen in the heavens. There will be the coalescing of a destructive comet with this conglomerate mass of cosmic dust, which will eventually be a world.'

"The fiery monster looked to me like a horrible dragon, with body, head and legs a mass of sulphurous flame. The creature seemed to fill the whole heavens, and for a time obscured everything else from sight. It swept everything before it and drew everything behind it. I could feel the intense heat it caused, and I could see the clouds bursting apart as if torn by angry hands and then cast aside, after it had passed, to melt into a molten mass of fire behind that monster of the skies. Then came a fearful report. There had been a collision between the comet and the new center or world, and the crash was awful. After that there was darkness and silence, and my Master quickly took me away from the fearful scene. But I had learned something about focusing forces, which was of greater importance and would be of more assistance to me in my studies than anything I had ever before witnessed."

In the diary of the same student of Occultism, from which the above description was quoted, is another, concerning the destruction of an old, dead world, which illustrates the operation of the destructive forces that may also be sent from a cosmic Center of consciousness quite as well as the former description illustrated the operation of constructive power. Because of the limited space allotted to a lecture, only such excerpts will be used as will cast light directly upon the subject in hand.

"Millions of miles from our earth we saw a wondrous, brilliant light, and advancing toward it we discovered that it was not a sun, nor moon, nor globe, nor was it like any planet I had ever seen. It was egg-shaped, and gave forth a light greater and more refulgent than any flaming sun in all the Universe. It seemed like a monster arc-lamp with rays of blue electric light streaming forth from it in all directions, and, like the jagged lightning shooting from a summer thunder cloud, the destructive, forked tongues of its electric fire were sent forth and were divided into millions of flaming bolts that went speeding into space. And while I gazed upon it surprised and spellbound it suddenly, as if possessed with consciousness, drew within itself its dazzling light and assumed a greenish hue. It also shrank to half its former size, and, like a monster serpent, seemed to coil its forces for a spring, while in its center burned a dark red flame that at any moment was ready to burst forth and consume everything within its reach.

"A strange attraction drew me toward the monster light, and I had a most intense desire to know of what it was composed and what its mission was; for I have learned that no created thing can live and move without a purpose. Approaching nearer, I observed that the strange light had been created by the burning of what seemed to be great quantities of hydro-carbon vapor and aeriform matter. Numerous strong electric currents seemed to focus at that point, thus creating a generating center of magnetic force. Here was a Celestial Dynamo, and the heat caused by the intense vibrations of those powerful electric currents had produced a radiation sufficient to ignite the gases. Combustion was the result of this focusing, and was followed by the wondrous pyrotechnical display which we were witnessing.

"But where do those electric currents come from? I mentally inquired, and my Master replied: 'Look yonder,' and, looking, I saw far away in the heavens another great light. It appeared to be a group, of seven suns, with the colors orange, red, green, blue and yellow radiating from them. In the center of each of these suns was a spot of light of the color orange which deepened in shade towards its outer edge until it melted into a band of very dark red, color, which was green. Outside of the green was a broad band of blue, and outside of that there was a band of beautiful golden yellow. And as I watched that group of glorious suns I saw that from the broad belt of red so near the center of each, streamed the tremendous currents of light which focused at this point and producing this strange-looking center. This vortex was an evil-looking thing, and, although I seemed to know it was destructive in its nature, still I was attracted toward it, and had it not been for the restraining influence of my Master, I think I should have been inclined to approach too near.

"When I became satisfied in regard to the source

of those electric currents, I began to wonder for what
that Celestial Dynamo had been created, and then my
Master called my attention to a large, dark globe
so far away at that moment that it resembled a huge
black bird or a monster bat.   But as I continued to
watch its movements it came near enough for me to
see that it was a planet which seemed to be idly floating in space as a bit of driftwood floats upon the surface of a stream.

" 'May we not visit that globe or see its condition
from a closer point of view?' I asked, and for reply
my Master said : 'come,' and extended a hand to me.

"After a time we reached the queer old world and
stood among its ruins.   It was dead.   There was no
soil, no atmosphere, no life.   A deathly stillness
reigned; and on every side were dark, deep fissures,
into whose yawning depths I looked for many hundred feet.   The rough and rugged edges of those fissures showed that when that world was in the grasp
of death, when its life forces were taking final leave
of their material envelope, its surface was rent and
torn like thinnest gauze.   Even its mountains were
crushed and crumbled into hardened, blackened ash-
heaps, and, as I stood looking at that awful scene of
desolation, I saw at my left at a distance of a dozen
yards or more a monstrous hole — a well — which
seemed to reach to the very center of that globe.   And
its melted, lava-coated walls showed that it was but
one of the many outlets for the fires and gaseous

flames which had burst forth and swept that old planet in its last awful conflagration.

"Blackened and seared was everything. Not a drop of water was to be seen. Not a human habitation. Not an indication that animal or vegetable life had ever existed there. It was most evident that the planet had served its purpose, had lived its time, and, becoming useless, was robbed of all its wealth, and it now remained a huge ball of crumbling coke; for what had been once a soil of moist earth was now a hardened porous crust.

"In my intense interest I did not think there was danger in our remaining upon that old sphere, and would have been glad to wander up and down its strange formations. I wanted to explore the well, and was about to descend when my Master said: 'If you are satisfied we will retire and watch the coming dissolution at a distance,' and, taking my hand, we left the place and stationed ourselves sufficiently far away to enable us to watch the destruction which seemed imminent. Soon we saw the dead world commence to move in great, wide circles round the evil-looking vortex. Sometimes it paused, swaying and trembling as it felt the drawing power of that great vortex. And then it would dart away as if for a little the attractive force were broken and it were free again. But then came renewed activity at that flaming center of attraction. It assumed a darker, redder hue, and like a great unwinking eye seemed to be watching for its helpless victim to draw near.

Again the old world was caught by the attracting power of its enemy and was whirled round and round like a tiny boat within a boiling maelstrom. With every revolution it gradually drew nearer and nearer to that fiery center until there was a terrific roaring sound like a thousand cataracts blended into one. At times the noise was like the booming of a fearful cannonade. Sometimes there seemed to be something like shrieking, bursting shells sent forth from that fiery center, and then again there were streams of jagged lightning which sent destructive bolts of fire and smashed the surface of that globe as if it were an egg-shell.

"It was celestial war that we were witnessing, and if all the battles that were ever fought upon our tiny earth were combined into one it could not compare with this destruction. As we watched its progress I remembered what was written in the Book of Revelation, in the twelfth chapter, and the seventh verse: 'And there appeared another wonder in heaven; and behold a great red dragon, having seven heads and ten horns * * * and his tail drew the third part of the stars of heaven and did cast them to the earth.'

"Here were destructive forces at work, and while we watched and listened to the fearful, crushing, grinding sound they made, the dark red center of light turned almost black, and then came the awful final crash. It seemed as though the whole heavens had become suddenly filled with sulphurous fire; the monster eye was now a blazing demon bursting with terrific power, and then it seized that helpless globe and ground it into powder.

"The work of destruction was almost finished. Compared with what it had been, the blackened ball was now a speck; and encircled as it was with flame, we saw it disappear and become dispersed into clouds of dust. Then the flames began to fade, and we realized that the fires in that celestial crematorium were going out. The atoms of a dead and useless world were scattered through space, and became again a part of the differentiated portion of God.[1]

"As we started to return to earth I asked my Master what had become of the fiery destructive center—for it had then entirely disappeared—and he replied: 'What becomes of the flame when the gas is turned off? or what becomes of the cyclone when the wind ceases to blow?'

"Then I understood that the seven Elohim or Planetary Spirits who had combined into a group to generate and to send forth Their electric forces, had withdrawn them when the old world corpse had been destroyed, and I wondered if I could be wise enough to apply the lesson I had just learned from cosmos, to the removing of rubbish from my mundane path in life."

The power that operates through great centers also operates through small ones; and thus man, with his physical body, generates within himself, although to a lesser degree, the same power that manifests either

---

[1] The History and Power of Mind, p. 105.

constructively or destructively among comets, suns and worlds.

Like vibration, power cannot be qualified as either good or bad; but the manner in which it is expressed, and the centers through which it operates, are what determine the results of its action. And it is the results produced by its manifestation which determine whether it has been used or misused. It is often said of a person that he or she possesses an evil power, which statement is incorrect, since it is impossible for power to be evil.[1] It is possible, however, for a person temporarily to produce a so-called evil as the result of the misuse of his power. So long as a person or a nation continues to grow greater socially, politically or financially it is believed that he or it is sustained by a good power. This is evidence of the sub-conscious race belief that construction of form is always good and that destruction of form is always bad. Only to a certain degree is this belief true, for it should be remembered that when old forms of government, old social customs and old financial methods have served the time and purposes for which they were created, they must be destroyed as forms because they then limit instead of increase the opportunities for a higher expression of power. With individuals it is the same. The man who has used his physical body for one hundred years becomes limited in his expression of power, unless he is an advanced ego and knows how to rejuvenate and keep his physi-

---

[1]The History and Power of Mind, pp. 147-148.

cal form in working order. And even if he is able to renew his body by replacing many of his old atoms with new ones there will come a time when the power he generates as a center of consciousness requires an entire new form as an instrument of expression, and in a case of this kind the destruction of a physical form is not to be in the least regretted. It is the destruction of forms before they have served their purposes which is to be deplored, and a destruction of this kind the Occultist calls a misuse of power.

It was not a misuse of power when the Elohim or seven great centers of consciousness focused Their forces for the destruction of the old dead globe that was floating uselessly about in space, after its purpose had been served, any more than it was a misuse of power to focus Their forces upon the construction of the new world They desired to build. It was the same power used in both instances, but it was the mode of expression and consequent results that differed.

A center for the generation of power is and must be of a circular or slightly oval shape. This is a necessary condition in order that there may be no angles to obstruct the rotary motion necessary to generation. And this is as true of the atom as it is of suns and worlds and men. The physical body of man, which is but the material or external manifestation of him, is in something of a cylindrical form, while he himself is of an oval or egg shape; and he generates his individual force as do the atoms of which he is composed, by the constant rotary motion of the cosmic forces within him.

At the moment that the tiny human embryo is conceived, some of the orange life force which surrounds and permeates this planet rushes into it, and there continues the same rotating motion within that tiny center of life that it made around the earth; and at that moment the individual force of that new form is established.   Then its force increases in volume as the size of the center becomes enlarged, and the center is constantly being expanded under the force which is generated within it, until it can no longer remain in its pre-natal condition and, through its increased individual force, is expelled from its mother's womb.   Liberated from the narrow confines of the uterus and thus becoming capable of greater expansion, that generating center of force very soon begins to use its powers destructively.   This is because destruction is easier to accomplish than construction; and the human baby, like all other ignorant creatures of the animal kingdom, begins to express its powers in the manner easiest for it.

As the child continues to expand as a conscious center it begins to generate mental as well as physical force, and then it commences to use its forces constructively as well as destructively.   In its effort toward character building it first begins to imitate, and before it has grown to manhood or womanhood, it has become a center of conscious power capable of using not only the orange life force, with which it began life, but also the red, the green and the blue cosmic forces. And it is through the use of these that it evolves still greater power. If it uses these cosmic forces unconsciously its power will be expressed physically more than mentally; but if it uses them consciously through the power of concentration, then even the physical forces emanating from that center will be strengthened and controlled by its greater mental powers.

Concentration of thought is essential to the generation of mental force, for without it mental creations cannot exist long enough to become materialized.[1] The man who does not concentrate his thoughts upon what he wishes to do never does anything well. He is always an unreliable and an unsatisfactory person, and is neither a good lover nor a good hater. He forgets to do what he should do and only does that which should not be done. He loses his own material possessions and scatters everything that has been entrusted to his care by others. He is always too late for his train and his meals; he either over-sleeps or does not sleep enough, because he has not the power to concentrate his thoughts.

For individualized centers of human force who need knowledge along this line a few examples in concentration will be given. Concentration of thought means the power to think of one thing to the exclusion of all other things. To conserve energy—which is force—it is always better to concentrate upon

---

[1]The History and Power of Mind.—Lecture Seven.

something which may be of use rather than upon an object that is of no use, such as a spot on the wall or a cloud in the sky. Some students of Eastern Occultism are taught to concentrate upon their navel or upon the end of their nose.

Unless a student understands what his navel is and what it is for, and that the forces he generates pass down his left side into his lower extremities and up the right side, through his brain, then down the left side to his feet again and up and around and around his navel, there is not much good to be gained by concentrating upon his navel. But if he can picture or see the forces at work within him, and if he can realize that the navel is a center of consciousness in his body, that it is the largest magnetic center for the generation of physical force that he possesses then it is a very good thing for him to concentrate his thoughts upon. For, under these mental conditions his physical forces will be strengthened by the mental concentration. But there is nothing to be gained by concentrating the thoughts upon the end of one's nose, unless perhaps it should be an elongation of that particular feature, which to most persons is not desirable. It is better to select something to practise with which it is desirable to possess, then the force is not wasted, since every thought sent out to a particular thing carries with it a little magnetic thread, and, when the thought fastens upon the object concentrated upon, a magnetic connection is immediately made between it and the mind that sent it. This thread attracts because it is of the nature of a magnet. It draws and will continue to draw to the person the object he is concentrating upon until it will finally become an actual possession of his own.

There are three planes of being to be drawn from, the material, the mental and the spiritual, and an example will be given for each. In order that a student should be able to do his best work in concentration he should first become conscious of his needs. It is when the heart longs most earnestly for a thing that the mind makes the best mental picture of it. Concentration is not an artificial or an unnatural, mental or physical condition; it is simply looking, with the physical eyes either open or closed, at one thing without seeing any other.

If a thinly clad man is passing along the street on a cold, windy day and suddenly sees a warm, comfortable-looking overcoat in a tailor's window, involuntarily he stops and concentrates his thoughts upon it. There may be one hundred other things in that same window, such as neckties, opera hats, light gloves and evening suits, but he does not see anything except the overcoat of which he is painfully in need. His eyes are open, and to a person watching him it would seem as if he were carefully scrutinizing the entire contents of the window when he really sees nothing but the one garment. This is physical and mental concentration combined.

It was not a difficult thing to do, and the man did it without realizing that he was concentrating.

He was interested in what he was concentrating upon, and therefore it was a pleasant rather than an unpleasant mental exercise. But if he had possessed six overcoats it would have been impossible for him to stand before that window and look at the inside without noticing some of the other things that were with it. He would have seen most clearly the things that he most needed.

If a woman has lost her health and her youth; if she is old and wrinkled and white-haired; even if she is in possession of many material things, or if she stands ever so high in the social world, she is nevertheless painfully in need of the things which she has not. In her heart she desires to be young and well and beautiful. And when she hears her joints creak as she attempts to rise from her chair she very naturally thinks of the time when she danced and ran or skipped the rope with the other girls. In her mind rises the picture of herself as she looked then, with her rosy cheeks and bright eyes and with her hair falling in a mass of tangled curls to her waist. She is concentrating upon a mental picture because the material picture has disappeared, and, unconsciously, she is feebly using a means by which she might regain the youth and health she once possessed, if she knew how to use her mental powers rightly. If, after looking at the mental picture of herself as she once was, and would like to be again, she goes to her mirror and gazes at the gray hair and wrinkled face and bent figure that is there reflected and says: "Oh, yes, I am an old woman with one foot in the grave, and I never can be any better in this world," then by that very declaration and by her acceptance of the unfortunate situation, she destroys the good results which would have come from concentrating upon her first mental picture. But if she would keep away from her mirror for one year and permit her maid to arrange her toilet and her hair; and if she would continue to hold that beautiful mental picture of herself without thinking of age and ill-health, she would find at the end of that time that she was growing younger instead of older. And if she would include physical exercise and plenty of fresh air with her mental picture of herself, as she was when she was young, she would make tremendous strides up the mountain of life instead of down into the valley, with its shadows, tears and despair. As an aid to a woman's mental concentration for youth, all mirrors should be removed from her apartments.

But suppose a person has all the material things he needs—money, home and friends. And suppose he has not become aged and ill, but is in possession of the vigor and strength of middle age and desires mental and spiritual power more than anything else in the world. He reads everything he can find written about the great minds who have lived on earth; and he concentrates his thoughts for hours at a time upon the wonderful work they did; and he reverentially wishes or demands that such mental and spiritual power as they possessed should come to him. He reads

of the Masters and the Saviors of mankind, and longs
to know something of their occult methods of control-
ling the elements and of producing harmony where
disharmony prevailed.   Unconsciously to himself,
perhaps, that person is demanding to be omniscient
and omnipotent.   But if he follows his mental demands with a conscious drawing into himself of the
blue and the yellow cosmic currents, which are the
mental and spiritual portions of Divine Mind, then
he is scientifically working with vibratory law.[1]   If,
while he concentrates his thoughts upon his ideals, he
is conscious of the fact that he, too, is a center for
the generation of mental and spiritual power, and
watches the mental and spiritual forces as they cir-
culate round and through his body and brain, he must
inevitably gain the wisdom and power that he desires
because he is using the law which governs the generation of mental and spiritual power.

But it should be remembered that this can be accomplished only by the ego who undertakes it because
he desires to become omniscient and omnipotent.   If
mental and spiritual growth are his coveted treasures he will gain them through his own power of
concentration and generation, and in no other way.

---

[1]The History and Power of Mind, pp. 158-160; 235-238.

LECTURE SEVEN.

MENTAL REPULSION.

"In the beginning was the Word. * * * and the Word was God. * * * The same was in the beginning with God. In him was life; and the life was the light of men. And the light shineth in the darkness; and the darkness comprehended it not."

Before the existence of motion or vibration there was "the Word" (Divine Will), and it was because Divine Mind put Divine Will into operation that motion—vibration—began in the Universe. As Divine Will is the cause of vibration, so vibration is also the generator or creator of the force that manifests as attraction and repulsion. And it is upon the operation of this force, generated by vibration, that the perpetuation of form depends. Since form is essential to manifestation, and since form could not exist without vibration, then vibration is the keynote of creation, and without it the manifested portion of the Universe would cease to manifest.

The creation of a form begins with the amalgamation of two or more atoms which are vibrating at the same common rate. And the growth of a form is due to the continuous attraction of more atoms of a rate common to that nucleus or center. For example:

The first tiny leaf with its stem that appears above the soil, as it springs forth from the acorn embedded in the earth, is a nucleus for an oak tree; and it will continue to grow because of its power of attraction. The attractive force is as dependent for its existence upon the vibration of the atoms it draws together to enlarge the form through which it works, as the form is dependent upon the force for its growth. And thus the power and the center each grow in strength and size with every added atom. This force is attractive only to such atoms as are vibrating at a common rate with those which compose its center of operations; and it is as forcefully repellent to all other atoms as it is attractive to those of its selection. It is for this reason that all the leaves appearing upon that particular form or manifestation of force are similar in construction, and that the wood composing the trunk and limbs of that particular tree is similar in its consistency. If it were not possible for the force operating through that center to repel the wrong atoms as strongly as it attracts the right ones, then that center would have no distinct character of its own, but would be composed of any kind of atoms and would be as likely to have a part of its limbs of pine or of hemlock as of oak. And its body would be as apt to be composed of ash and of maple as of anything else.

It is in the same manner that the vibratory law manifests in every sphere or plane in the Universe. In the mineral and animal kingdoms it works with a distinct purpose the same as in the vegetable kingdom. Among the minerals the atoms which vibrate at a rate manifesting as gold are attracted and adhere together as gold; and, as a center of force, it has a character and a value separate and distinct from any other metal or mineral.

The vibration of the atoms composing a center in the animal kingdom are of a much higher rate than are those of the mineral or vegetable kingdom, and, since it is in accordance with the law of vibratory attraction that force grows stronger with the increase of the power of its center, the force manifesting as attraction and repulsion in an animal or a man is much greater than in either of the lower kingdoms. In these higher forms of manifestation this force is not confined to the selection and rejection of physical atoms that will compose its material center, but it goes a step further and manifests also as mental likes and dislikes. For a law of physics is also a law of metaphysics, and the law of attraction and repulsion operates more forcefully and with greater rapidity upon the mental than upon the material plane, and this is because of the higher rate of vibration of the atoms composing mind or soul. The objective mind of man, being of a lower rate of vibration than the subjective mind, is more repellent than attractive to the things which would serve to aid man in his evolutionary journey. And it is because man permits his objective mind to direct his affairs for him, that he meets with so much sorrow and disharmony in physical life. Before the Sons of God or subjective minds came to earth to incarnate in animal forms, they were negatively good in the realm of innocence in which they dwelt and therefore they enjoyed a negative happiness there. But when they undertook the task of incarnating upon this earth in the physical forms that were already under the control of positive animal minds, they were as utterly unable to control them at first as a child is unable to control a man. And while those subjective minds were becoming accustomed to their new environment they were entirely under the dominion of their objective or lower minds.

During all the ages that have passed since the Sons of God came here to dwell, a few have gained absolute control over their objective minds and have therefore evolved beyond the condition of the mass of humanity, which is still suffering under that dominion. Those few souls have the freedom of thought and action that are the attributes of spiritual men and are now positively happy because of their positive goodness; and they have evolved to the point where they are no longer the victims of circumstances, but absolutely control their environment. There are others who have not yet reached the point of development where they are able constantly to control their animal or objective minds, but who are trying to do so, and it is to such egos that the message of occultism is given.

In Lecture Five of this Course a description was given of the origin and development of man's objective mind; in Lecture Six it was shown that man is a center for the expression of force and by reason of this, he belongs either to the constructive or to the destructive side of nature. If he is destructive he uses the destructive forces of nature, since those are the forces he attracts to himself by reason of his own rate of vibration. If his animal mind dominates his actions then he, as a center or vortex, draws to himself force from the cosmic currents out of which his animal mind was created. And since that mind was formed of the orange, the red and the green currents blended together, those three are the forces which he uses.[1] The orange life force supplies his body with physical strength. From the red cosmic force he draws his different emotions and passions and by its aid he hates and quarrels and destroys his own and other persons' property. Through the use of this current he is immoral and irregular in his habits. He indulges his appetites and his sexual passions to a state of satiety, and, by reason of his excesses, precipitates upon himself the calamities and misfortunes which are the natural consequences of such indulgence.

By aid of the green cosmic force he becomes more individualized in the misuse of his forces. Where once he raised a mob of men to help fight his battles, he now challenges other men to fight duels, and where he once was quite content to satisfy his sexual desires by indulgence with almost anything in female

---

[1] The History and Power of Mind, pp. 224; 228-238.

form, he now prefers a mistress or mistresses of his own.

Where by aid of the red force alone he once robbed and took by physical force the property and rights of others and then scattered his ill-gotten gains as quickly as he had secured them, he, through the added power of the green force, now desires aggrandizement. He robs and steals in secret and then protects and continues to hold the property he has gained by making laws, or by bribing law makers to favor him in his dishonesty.

As a natural consequence the mental condition of such a man is one of constant repulsion to certain persons and certain things; and the forces which manifest through him as a center are generally destructive and repulsive. Because of his disregard of the voice of conscience, his subjective mind has very little influence over him for the betterment of his condition; and instead of progressing mentally or physically, he becomes more and more hampered and harassed by the troubles of his own creation. After many lives of this kind he has accumulated karmic debts which are like millstones about his neck, limiting his power and even his desire to demand good for himself. He finds no one who can or will trust or believe in his promises because he has been and is so untrustworthy. He repels mentally and physically other persons who are better developed and more refined than himself. Because of his grossness and vulgarity, he attracts to himself as his friends only those who are at the same common rate of mental vibration with himself, and this is because only such persons can endure his vibrations. It is not at all helpful to him to have such undeveloped people as these for his friends, since, like himself, they, too, are seeking aggrandizement and wish to use him as a means to further their ends. They will profess friendship for him so long as he can be made of use, but when he refuses to accede further to their demands these friends immediately become his enemies.

Because of the wrongs committed in lives previous, he will sometimes be compelled to live in the closest family relationship with persons whom he hates and who hate him. And because of his environment, which he knows not how to change, he is sometimes compelled to live thus and suffer for a lifetime without relief. For example: Here is an ego incarnated in female form. For many lives in succession, whether with a masculine or feminine personality, she has given expression only to her selfish, animal desires. She is now born into a family with several brothers and sisters who are all younger than herself. She is without financial means and lives in a locality where there are no opportunities for her to gain money. Her parents are poor, her relatives are poor and all her neighbors are poor. The great Karmic Law has now placed her where she cannot steal as in her former lives, because there is nothing here that is worth stealing. She cannot improve herself socially or financially at another's expense, because there is nothing in that environment for a social or financial foundation. She is obliged to cook and wash and iron for the different members of her family because there is no one else to do it. Her brothers and sisters and the father and mother for whom she toils do not show her any affection and she is in such a repellent mental condition, because of her unhappy environment, that she naturally repels all affection. And because of the hatred and bitterness in her heart she is in a constantly inharmonious condition. This condition repels every good thing that might come to her, and attracts things which are of a similar inharmonious and destructive vibration. Because she has no knowledge of the justice of the great Law, she is forced to believe in luck and declares that she has nothing, and does not expect to have anything but bad luck for the remainder of her life. She becomes pessimistic about everything. If she lives on a farm and her family depends for their maintenance upon what can be raised there, she predicts frosts to kill, floods to drown, and fires to burn everything they possess. And since it is in accordance with law that what one really expects will surely come, this pessimistic, inharmonious, fearing woman's life becomes a continuous disappointment.

If she plans to go somewhere, as a preface, she declares that it will storm before she returns and ruin her clothes and her pleasure. She thinks storm and watches for it, and it is pretty sure to come and do all the mischief that she declared or thought it would do. It was not because she had the mental power to bring a storm through her pessimistic thinking, but she was drawn into the storm because it was an inharmonious condition of the elements and vibrated at the same common rate with her stormy, discordant mental condition.

This woman rebels against the "fate" which compels her to scrub and cook for the members of her family, and to one not acquainted with the operation of the Law of Justice, it would seem as if she were suffering from an injustice. But had she a memory of some of her past lives in all their fullness, she would know that the persons, whom she is now serving, are the same individuals to whom she owes debts. There is a brother whose heavy, coarse garments she is now obliged to wash and mend and whose stockings she must knit, in another life she either robbed outright of his money or borrowed it from him and never repaid. With the selfishness still in her nature that prompted her to do that wrong to him in another life, she would not willingly repay him in this life, even if she had the means, and so the great Law makes her serve him with her hands and feet until that debt is fully cancelled. There is a sister whose dresses she is obliged to make, and, for whom, after the daily household duties are done, she sometimes sits late into the night sewing and mending. It is true that she rebels against the work and hates her sister; and perhaps she even wishes that she could die and thus be rid of the burden. But she will never be rid of it until her karmic debt is fully paid. She does not know, and perhaps she does not care to know, what caused her bondage to that sister. But if she could look back into the past she might see that there was once a time when that individual, for whom she is now toiling, had been her servant whom she refused to pay. Because of the selfishness in her heart she took the service of that person's hands and feet and gave her nothing in return. She cheated her of the money she toiled for and used it for her own selfish purposes; but now the great Law of Justice has placed her where she must serve out this debt and she will never be released until it is paid. And so it is with every member of her family. She owes each one a debt that she is paying with her services, and it might be a temporary comfort to her troubled soul if she could but understand that it is not a cruelty but a kindness to have this opportunity in which to pay all these debts at once, instead of being obliged to take a lifetime for each.

But until her karmic debts are nearly paid she cannot see nor be made to understand either the cause of her condition or a way to get out of it. In her repellent mental attitude she cannot and will not accept nor believe in the law of Demand and Supply. This is because her karma is as yet but partly exhausted. There are so many remaining karmic debts between her and the light of freedom that they obscure that light from her vision, as the rain clouds obscure the sun from the earth. The woman cannot accept so high a truth as this, but instead will attract to her mind many superstitions and false beliefs. This is because these untruths are vibrating in harmony with her own false, untruthful nature; and, as the force working through the oak tree attracts only such atoms as are needed to build the oak and to give it its oaken character and repels all other atoms, so does this woman attract such beliefs or superstitions as correspond with her nature and her mental vibrations.

Humanity as a mass cannot receive or understand the higher Occult Truths. It is only the few who are consciously working to control their objective minds who are ready to be helped at the present time in this way. These lessons are written for the few who desire to become practical Occultists, the first three lectures of this course are the foundation stones of Adeptship, and no one will ever be accepted as a student by the Silent Brotherhood who does not build his character upon them.[1]

Before the subjective minds of animal men have become to any degree victorious over their objective minds, the superstitions created by their animal hopes and fears are the only things that they can understand or appreciate. To the undeveloped, ignorant, animal-man's mind the howling of a lonely dog at the hour of midnight is a warning that death is near; and he at once begins to wonder if it is his own death that is approaching. And for many days and sometimes for weeks afterward his thoughts may be so engrossed

---

[1] The History and Power of Mind, pp. 186-187.

with the fear of death that he stops swearing and drinking and behaves much better than for years. To the ignorant mind of an animal-woman who hears the faint ticking sound that is sometimes made by a little beetle as it burrows into the wooden wall, it is a sign of immediate death. Her particular superstition teaches that this sound is the death watch and is ticking away the seconds of her life; and she immediately turns her thoughts away from her gossiping and mischief making and begins preparations for her demise. But to the person who rules the objective mind, neither of these superstitions means anything, because he knows that he can control his own destiny and can use his physical body as long as he desires. And if he knew that the transition called death were near at hand, and if he believed it to be advisable for him to make the change, he would not be frightened into any better conduct because of it, since he lives each day to his highest ideal and therefore each day he is on his best behavior.

There is much confusion of thought concerning the operation of the Law of Demand and Supply in connection with the Law of Justice. In the Eastern School of Occultism the Karmic Law is so forcefully presented that it almost assumes an aspect of fatalism, or of "Kismet," as it is called by the Mohammedan. But the Western student is taught that the Law of Karma is a part of the Law of Demand and Supply. For example: Here is a man who is suffering from poverty. He seems to be unable to get a position by which he may earn his living. Every position that he applies for has been filled and perhaps in less than an hour before. He seems to be always too late for everything he wants, and he walks the streets praying for (demanding) work until he becomes so tired and faint from hunger that he can scarcely move or stand. He does not know, and perhaps would not believe it if he were told, that this is a karmic condition which is the result of his past demands for idleness. In another life, or during the earlier part of this one, he did not want work, but preferred idleness, and resented all suggestions of work when they were made to him. At that time he may have had plenty of means and did not need a position and he may then have vehemently declared that "the world owed him a living," and yet was not wise enough then to follow that absurd remark with the declaration that the world must pay its debt by giving him a living. This man is now suffering past karma which is really the supply of his demand for idleness. The earnest demands he now makes for work will bring future karma, in the form of work, and perhaps a great deal more than he can do; and when that times comes, if he has then learned something about the Law of Karma, he will wonder what he ever did to create a condition which brought such an amount of labor for him.

Here is another example: There are two brothers and both are suffering from illness and poverty. They are fond of each other and live harmoniously together, but there seems to be no way for them to get out of their unpleasant environment and both become greatly discouraged. One day one of the brothers finds a book in the road and takes it home to read. In that book is a statement of the Law of Demand and Supply and there are also rules for overcoming or "demonstrating" over poverty and disease, all of which appeal to him as true. He tells his brother about the book and declares his intention to put the rules into immediate practice. His brother cannot appreciate the teachings of the book, nor does he care to understand it, nor will he even listen while it is read to him. But the progressive brother continues to read and to think and commences to practice with the knowledge he gains. As a result he begins to overcome or demonstrate over his physical and financial difficulties and after a time rises superior to them while the other brother continues to be ill and poor and wretched. The poor brother refuses to help himself or to be helped by "such nonsense," and as the progressive brother's mental and physical vibrations grow higher because of his improved mental and physical conditions, the poor brother turns from him in bitterness of thought and perhaps grows to hate him because he is left behind in his undevelopment. The heart of the progressive brother is troubled because of the other one's mental attitude and wonders if this condition is karmic.

It is karmic; but it is a karma produced by the working of the Law of Demand and Supply. Both men were in their unhappy condition as a result of transgressing the law in another life. But the more progressive man had more nearly expiated his mistakes than had the other, and, when almost at the end of his karmic afflictions, his demand for relief was met by the great Law in the form of the book. He was far enough out from his karmic gloom to be able to see the truth when it was presented to him, and to profit by it. The other man, who would not listen, had not yet finished with his karma; there were still so many obligations to be paid that the shadows cast by them were too dense for him to see the truth. He was not ready and would not be until he had finished or had nearly finished with his expiation, after which he could be helped, as his progressive brother had been. But it might not be in this life and if that were the case those brothers had come to the parting of their ways And however sad it might seem to either it was inevitable. The difference in the mental and physical vibrations of each would separate them as surely as oil separates from water, and this separation would come because of the action of the law of vibration.

Thus it may be stated as a rule that when a person accepts the Law of Demand and Supply as a truth, it is an indication that his old karma is nearly exhausted and that he is then in a position to demand and very soon to enter a better environment. But when a person closes his eyes and ears to this truth, and refuses to accept or consciously to make use of the Law of Demand and Supply, it is an indication that he has a large amount of old karma to overcome and that he cannot get out, nor be helped out of his unhappy condition until those karmic debts are paid.

There are several very important conditions to be observed when a student commences consciously to use the Law of Demand and Supply; for it is one thing to use it unconsciously as do the plants and animals and many men, and another thing to use it consciously. The first step is to learn all that is possible about it by studying its operations and by tracing the causes for existing conditions in one's self and in others. If a person is in possesion of something which he does not desire and which he seems to be unable to get rid of, he should first concentrate his thoughts upon it and demand to know how it came into his possession and what he did to bring it. And when he is perfectly satisfied that he does not and never will want that thing again, then he should concentrate his mind upon it and demand that it shall be removed.

The man of regular, orderly habits, who never drinks liquor nor smokes tobacco in any form, sometimes wonders, with indignation, why persons make him presents of bottles of wine and boxes of cigars. He should not permit himself to become indignant, because, either in a former life or in the earlier part of this one, he wanted or demanded and used these things which now he cares nothing for; and wine, pipes and cigars are the supplies which are still coming in answer to his former demands. In the next life, because of the indignation he now feels when such things are presented to him, he will probably be so situated that he could not get a bottle of wine if he should want it, and pipes, tobacco and cigars will also be great rarities.

Time given to concentration is never wasted. Many persons are inclined to consider this mental work an interruption to legitimate business. But all business, as well as every kind of pleasure, is better done and more satisfaction is derived from doing it, if concentration of thought is brought to bear upon it. The successful person concentrates his mind upon everything he does. He never decides a question without deliberation and the greater and deeper the concentration he gives to it the better and more satisfactory are his results. It is the same when making a demand for the more concentration put upon that demand and the more time given to it the sooner it will be met.

The reason one person has more power of concentration than another is because he has had more practice. This may be due to the fact that he is an older ego, or it may be because he has improved his time better.

If a person is so situated that all his material wants are supplied he is not inclined to demand or to concentrate upon them, but he then has a good opportunity to demand and to concentrate upon mental and spiritual power. If he does this he is improving his time and is gaining in the power of concentration the same as is the man who demands and concentrates upon material things; for the power of concentration increases with use, and whether it is used for a higher or a lower purpose it must and will grow. And the demands made for things that are injurious to both the body and the mind of a man will be met through his power of concentration just as surely as will the demands for things which will raise him materially, mentally and spiritually.

For example: He who concentrates his thoughts upon the creation of a system by which he may break the bank at Monte Carlo may use the same amount of concentration upon his demand for knowledge along this line that another man might use in studying how to make the lens of a telescope that would enable astronomers to know the actual climatic and atmospheric conditions of the planet Mars. The power of concentration of each of these men would develop equally while they were studying their different subjects and thus they would have, and be ready to use, that power at another time upon some other demand which would be of greater personal value to each. And here again the Law of Karma comes into operation. The reason the man wishes to break the bank at Monte Carlo is because, either in this life or in another, he has been robbed of every dollar he possessed by that or by some other gambling institution. In his heart he has a desire to retaliate for the material loss he has sustained through gaming, and uses his power of concentration in this manner. The time he spends in concentrating is not wasted because he has gained in power thereby, but the karma he makes for himself by hating and demanding revenge will tie him for another life perhaps to the men whom he now seeks to injure. Knowing this, it is wiser to select as a subject for concentration things or qualities that will be of benefit rather than a detriment.

Here is a man who greatly desires to gain a knowledge of medicine. He longs for the time to come when he can devote his entire time to this study. But he has now neither the means nor the opportunity. He lives in a rural district and is obliged to rise at four or five o'clock in the morning to milk the cows. He has not a moment of time to read until after the last duty has been done at night when he may take an hour perhaps to study the advertisements for patent medicines in the weekly newspaper. Yet his mind is filled with the desire to go to college and to become a practising physician. And it may be that nothwithstanding his longing and demand for this knowledge, he may not have it met in this life because of his unfavorable karmic conditions, and because of his lack of knowledge of the Law of Demand and Supply. If he could know that the demands he is now making will be met in his next life just as surely as these obstacles which are now in his way were put there by demands made in another life, he would be better satisfied to wait. During some other life he desired to possess the farm and the stock which now stand in the way of his study of medicine; and he demanded that kind of work then just as earnestly as he is now demanding a college education.

When he has gained all the experience that he needs from his old demands, when he knows all that is necessary about farming and stock raising, then his condition will change, and in his next incarnation he may be born the son or daughter of an eminent physician, and in his new environment have every opportunity to study, which is now denied him. The more concentration he puts on his farming now the more power of concentration will he possess as a physician, and the better work will he do then.

It is impossible to utterly fail in demonstrating for even the lightest wish, if not destroyed by an equally strong denial, will some time bring the thing wished for. But it may not come at the time it is desired, or perhaps for a long time after the desire for it is dead; but it must and will come some time, when the vibrations of the individual who wished for it have been changed from repulsion to attraction.

A pessimistic condition of mind is always the cause of mental and physical repulsion of good things. The person who can only see disaster and destruction before him, draws those conditions into his life the same as the happy, hopeful mind draws peaceful and beautiful things into his life. The pessimist selects the misfortunes as forcefully as he rejects the blessings of life, and because he receives what he selects or demands, he is unhappy and makes every one round him so. The pessimistic man in business, whether he be a merchant, a banker, a broker, or an investor, is always losing his money. He expects to lose it, and therefore the Law gives him the opportunity. Because he believes all men are dishonest he is drawn into business transactions with dishonest men only. He lives and moves in the destructive current of dishonesty, and if he does not get out of his unfortunate mental condition, he will never succeed in anything he undertakes. Pessimism, like any other defect of character, increases with every moment of time that it is permitted to influence a person's actions. But if it does not find an external means of expression, like any other weed in the heart garden, it will die.

The best manner by which a tendency to pessimism may be overcome is to set up an opposing current of vibration by reversing the expression of pessimistic opinion. If it looks as though it were going to rain, declare that the sun is coming out, and ignore, and if possible, forget the fact that the clouds are dark and threatening. If one feels miserable and wretched, one should search for the cause of the trouble. If it is found to be a torpid liver or a severe case of indigestion, change cooks or diet. If neither brings the desired relief, wash out the stomach and intestines with warm salt water and fast for a day or two. In the meantime go into the fresh air and sunshine. Take a trip out of town or visit some one who is jolly and good tempered. If the pessimistic condition is found to be caused by mental depression alone, then declare peace and happiness until they come and drive away the mood. If the pessimistic condition has come because of the loss of material things or of friends declare that no thing nor person can be lost to you that belongs to you. If what you supposed was yours belonged to some one else, you are glad that it has reached its real owner at last; then stop thinking about it and commence making demands for something else to take the place of that which has been taken from you.

Every ego is just where it belongs at this moment. And every ego will eventually become what it really desires to be. If it desires to grow and to progress, the opportunities will be given as fast as it can make use of them. But if it prefers to retrogress and degenerate, then abundant opportunities will be given to it; and if it persists in retrogression and never progresses then it will some time reach a point where the Great Consciousness will re-absorb it and it will cease to exist as an individualized center, and will be drawn back again into the atomic or differentiated portion of God—Divine Mind.

All the blossoms on the fruit trees do not become fruit. But none is wasted, because the Mother Principle in nature re-absorbs the blasted blossoms, and the same power of selection which drew to the tree the atoms which gave it power to bring forth the first flowers will draw back to it the atoms that are scattered round it upon the earth. And when the next season comes blossoms will again appear, stronger and more beautiful than the others, because of the added force the tree has gained through their absorption.

Discouragement is but a step above pessimism. And when one yields to and remains in a discouraged condition of mind over seeming failures to make demonstrations, he has temporarily, at least, entered the destructive mental current with the pessimist. Discouragement repels good things, and, like pessimism, attracts the undesirable. It is born of impatience, and it is because a person becomes impatient and unwilling to wait for his demands to be met that he becomes discouraged.

But if every Son of God could only realize that every wish he makes will some time be granted, and that, too, so soon as the avenue through which it must come shall be cleared of the thought rubbish he himself has placed therein, discouragement with him would die a natural death. Egos should look with broadened vision beyond this short life, which is but a day in the evolutionary journey of each.

The wise man who starts to take a trip around the world plans for more than a day at a time. He telegraphs ahead for his steamer and railroad accommodations, and if he fails to get them, he waits for others. And while waiting he gets as much enjoyment as possible out of his environment. If he were to rush and fume or get discouraged and turn back every time he missed a train or when a delay occurred, all enjoyment of his trip would be destroyed and his entire journey, which should be one of pleasure and profit, would become a continuous mental and physical strain —a wear and tear upon his nervous system.

If a person has demanded money he should wait until it comes before he spends it, and then he will have no debts to trouble him. It is always best to live within one's income and if possible have something left over each month or year to use in case an emergency should arise. It is the anxiety of not knowing how to meet one's financial obligations which causes the greatest discouragement in life. If a man is so situated that he cannot afford to live like a prince, then let him live in the manner befitting his station until his demands shall be met, when he will be able to live as he desires.

Learn to wait and to wait patiently, as God—Divine Mind—waits for the development of man.

LECTURE EIGHT.

MENTAL ATTRACTION.

In Lectures Six and Seven, vibration was described as the keynote of Creation, and sufficient was said to acquaint the student with its position as a pivotal element in the Universe. Limited space prevents a further discussion of vibration per se, but further information will be given regarding its influence upon the subjective mind and upon man's relationships in physical life.

In opposition to mental repulsion, disharmony and pessimism, or the destructive mental forces, are mental attraction, optimism and progression or the constructive mental forces. It is necessary to study both forces in order to gain a thorough understanding of the operation of the Law of Evolution, for the student must be shown the seamy or wrong side of life as well as the right or finished side.

The egg-shaped center of consciousness called mind or man is the highest vibrating center of force that continuously exists upon this planet as form. And it is only because of its union with the objective mind, and the preponderance of the objective mind, that the subjective mind is compelled to remain upon the earth. Being of a higher rate of vibration than the earth, or than anything produced by the earth, it could not be confined to this material plane if it were not for this union. And until the lower mind shall be raised and shall be made to vibrate in harmony with its higher mind, neither mind can progress beyond its present condition.

The animal mind is to the subjective mind what the anchor-drag is to the ship, or to the captive balloon. It holds its subjective mind upon this mundane sphere by means of the magnetic mental attraction that exists between them. And the objective mind, by reason of its greater weight or lower rate of vibrations, is held to the earth by its own density, and by its attraction to the material things upon the earth. And until the animal mind shall cease to love the things of earth, shall become less sensuous, and shall turn more of its attention toward mental and spiritual things, it will continue to be just what it is—a jailor for its subjective mind, who is now its most unhappy prisoner upon this plane.

Before coming into contact with its objective, animal mind, the subjective mind was happy and hopeful. It knew nothing of sorrow nor of disappointment, nor of the physical ills or troubles of material life. And when its mission upon this plane has been fulfilled, and it has so far conquered that lower, animal mind as to become its master instead of its slave, then its original nature will be reasserted and it will again be happy. When that great victory has been gained its happiness will be positive, that of a glorified ego rather than the negative happiness of a help-less, ignorant infant. Then its fetters of limitation will fall away, and, because of its spiritual knowledge and power, it will be able to pass at will beyond this vale of tears into the realm where there are no tears, and where physical and material troubles are never experienced. But before that great triumph can be gained there are many steps to be taken on its evolutionary journey; and the first of these is to acquire perfect poise.

Before the human child can walk or run it must learn to stand by gaining and maintaining its physical equilibrium; and what is true upon the material plane is also true upon the mental plane. After mental poise is acquired it must be maintained, since mental progression without poise is as impossible to attain as is physical progression without equilibrium.

In the ego's struggle for freedom fear is the first and last enemy that has to be overcome.[1] It is the most formidable attribute of the objective mind, and it is that which limits man to the narrowest confines of earth. So long as it rules and reigns in the human heart, mental poise and complete individualization are impossible to attain; for fear casts its malefic influence upon men and women alike, and it retards the growth of an ego more than does any other thing.

Physical fear and fear of loss are the first two aspects of this retarding influence to be overcome; and in order to accomplish this the ego must learn to

[1] The History and Power of Mind, pp. 72-73, 85, 140-141, 230.

recognize its own indestructibility. Composed as it is of ethereal substance of a higher rate of vibration than that of material things, it can neither be destroyed nor injured by material things, nor by the loss of material things, nor by the loss of friends. Since individualization is God's ultimate purpose for every ego, earthly transitions, such as the coming and going of friends or of enemies, can only hinder or help, according to the ability of a soul to keep its poise.

As an aid toward the recognition of its individuality an ego must first learn to be happy when alone, and not to be dependent upon another person or persons for its pleasure or happiness. It is the human baby that must be kept quiet and amused by a rattlebox or a bell, or by something that can make a noise or confusion. But when its physical body and brain have matured it should evolve beyond the necessity for rattleboxes and bells, and should be amused and entertained by thoughts instead of things. Not that man should cease to love the society of his friends, or that he should retire from this beautiful world with all its wonderful scenery; but he should not be dependent upon persons or things for his pleasure or his happiness.

The person who cannot be alone for a moment without being lonely or wretched, but who must have some one to talk to, has no mental poise and very little individuality. The person who dares not go to sleep without a light burning in his room has no mental force or mental equilibrium. The person who cannot be content unless he is plunged into social gaieties or is madly rushing from one fete to another is utterly and entirely upon the physical plane of being, and is dragging his helpless, unhappy subjective mind after him as mercilessly as a conquering general drags after him his captives of war.

The next aspect of fear to be overcome is the fear of public opinion or of criticism.[1] There are men who have such tremendous physical strength that they do not fear to combat either man or beasts; and yet they may be completely cowed by a sarcastic glance, a scornful smile, or a shrug of the shoulders given by some one whose admiration they desire to gain. With set teeth and unfaltering step those men would walk straight forward to meet death in battle, or would die at the stake without a moan of pain; but they could not bear ridicule, and perhaps would sacrifice their highest moral principles rather than be pronounced out of date.

For example: Mr. Blank is really fond of his wife and of his family, and prefers to spend his evenings at home; but Mr. Dash, whose admiration and respect Mr. Blank greatly desires to gain, is fond of nothing but "a good time." Mr. Dash invites Mr. Blank to go with him "and make a night of it," and he goes because he is afraid that if he should refuse the invitation his friend would call him "a back number." It is true that he is not happy for one moment of the

---

[1] The History and Power of Mind, pp. 86-87.

time he spends in dissipation, but he has not the courage or the mental poise to look Mr. Dash in the eyes and say, "I prefer to remain at home with my wife." He could not bear the ridicule that would be provoked among his acquaintances by this "out-of-date" position.

And it is the same kind of fear that casts its demoralizing influence upon Mrs. Blank when Mrs. Dash invites her to a theatre party and a supper afterward, and provides old Mr. Roué as her escort for the evening. Mrs. Blank would much rather go to the play with her husband, whom she really likes better than any one she knows, but she is afraid to refuse this invitation. She has not the mental poise to look Mrs. Dash in the face and say, "If your invitation does not include Mr. Blank I must decline it." She could not bear the disdainful curl of Mrs. Dash's lip, nor the pitying glances of her acquaintances after taking such a prudish position; and so she goes to the party and permits Mr. Roué to say and do many things which she would not like her husband to know about. She does not enjoy the party, although she makes a pretense of doing so, and after the farce is ended she returns home humiliated and ashamed of her conduct, and all because she feared to be called a "prude." And thus two souls are retarded in their growth because they fear ridicule. Each loses its poise and individuality because of that element of fear which has always been the direct cause of most of the misery and failures in physical life.

It is this attribute of the objective mind that paralyzes the power of the artist to sing or to act before the public. He fears criticism or ridicule, and, by yielding to the power of his fear, places himself in the very position he most dreads. Then there are other persons who fear bad luck and accidents. To the ignorant objective mind of man such calamities seem to drop upon him out of nothingness; and the cause of either seems as intangible and difficult to understand as is the "Causeless Cause," or a dispensation of Providence." Because of a lack of knowledge concerning the operation of the law of vibration, he does not know how to escape from his misfortunes, and as soon as he emerges from one mishap another comes upon him, and, because of his constant dread or fear of them, he has neither poise nor peace.

The best way to destroy fear is to become indifferent to, and to lose interest in, the miserable mental pictures that fear paints.[1] When man can recognize his own individuality, his indestructibility and his superiority as compared with his material environment, fear will wither and die out of his heart, since it can only live because of the existence and exercise of his lower emotions. The artist who works for the world's flattery or praise, more than to attain perfection in art, is stimulated by the emotion of personal vanity. He is striving to place himself before the world, and uses art as a means to elevate him above the heads of his competitors. And because of

---

[1] The History and Power of Mind, pp. 85-88, 92,-99, 140, 141.

this desire for personal laudation he suffers from and fears the criticism of the world. But if he is working to attain perfection instead of praise, then he becomes his own most severe critic and has no other critic to fear. He is grateful for honest criticism and for good suggestions, and his skill improves because he accepts and profits by them. He gains in character and poise as he becomes more and more indifferent to ridicule or disparagement; and he does not take the pleasure or displeasure of the world into his consideration.

Fear and falsity go hand in hand, and it is usually the man who has something to conceal who most fears criticism or ridicule. It may be that it is his ignorance which he fears will be exposed and laughed at; in which case it is his position before the world, which he is unworthily trying to maintain, that he fears he may lose. Or, if he has not yet reached the desired position, but hopes to do so, then he fears that criticism may prevent him from gaining that which does not belong to him and which he does not deserve. If he could only recognize the truth that he is an evolving ego trying to reach perfection in all things, instead of pretending that he is now perfect; and if he could also recognize his inherent divinity and his indestructibility, he could not lose his poise, because he would know that he could not fail to gain his own if he persisted in his endeavor.

With the progressive ego there is a direct reversal of this order of thought. Because he has ceased to love material things better than mental or spiritual qualities, he has no fear of losing his earthly possessions, and gives to each article its proper value and place in his estimation. Knowing that the world and all it contains is perishable and therefore transitory, he is wise enough to select his treasures, which are imperishable from the mental and spiritual planes of being. If he does not remember his soul name, he selects the one, which, of all the names he has ever heard, is the most beautiful to him; and when alone he calls himself by it. He places the greater part of his consciousness upon the mental plane by living in his thought creations. He depends upon his inspirations for pleasure and happiness rather than upon the dross and tinsel of material things. To him, because he is well poised, the kaleidoscopic scenes of the material world are but passing shows. They are things to look upon, but not to live upon.

Evolutionary work never needs to be protected by the ego who is doing the work : because it will outlive all petty ridicule or unkind criticisms that may be put upon it. And it will also outlive the personalities of those who condemn it. Truth can never be destroyed. For a time it may become obscured by falsehood and deceit, but it cannot die any more than the progressing ego can die who writes or speaks it.

Every ego should have its aim, its object in life; and that object should be its ideal for good, and it should work with all its earnestness to reach that ideal and to become a part of it. To gain and to maintain poise while working for its ideal it should constantly declare: "I am imperishable and indestructible, and there is nothing for me to fear."

The object in dwelling so long on the subject of fear is twofold. First, to show that most of the calamities which befall men are produced by the fear which is an attribute of the animal or objective mind, and, second, to emphasize the deterrent effect that fear has upon the evolution of humanity. The mind being magnetic draws to itself whatever it persistently dwells upon; and the calamities in life are drawn to man, through fear, by the law of attraction. This aspect of the operation of the law was fully presented in "The History and Power of Mind."

The three elements which constitute the Law of Success are, first, a clear mental image of the object to be attained; second, the condition of the mind while in pursuit of its object, and, third, the conservation of energy.

The Law of Attraction is a fundamental principle underlying the Law of Success, but it is not the only principle; and the inability to recognize this fact is the cause of many of the seeming failures in the operation of the law.

The shortest distance between two points is a straight line, and if a man has in view only his present position and an indefinite point to which he would attain, he cannot travel in a straight line or take the shortest route toward his object. Therefore, one should not strive for, or demand, a general success, but, after deliberate thought, should determine in what line of work he desires specific success and then work to attain it. This is the first element.

The second element is the mode of mind one should maintain while working for success. And it is here that mental attraction performs a most important part. An optimistic mode of mind brings success, because optimism is evolutionism and works with instead of against the Law of Success. It is but another name for progression, and the optimist is the soul who has gained his mental poise and can see physical life in all its vicissitudes under an optimistic light. He has reached a point of development where he can look unmoved and undisturbed upon the hurrying, worrying members of society who are frantically rushing about after some external thing to give them pleasure or happiness. The pessimist hates him because he has been disturbed by his vibrations. When optimistic thought comes into contact with pessimistic thought it has the same effect upon it that sunlight and pure air have upon a dungeon. The rapid rates of vibration of the sunlight and the oxygen dry the dampness which produced the mustiness and mould in the dungeon and raise them to higher rates of vibration. But the mould forms and the odor of mustiness are disturbed and destroyed by the change, and the creatures that were born and bred in the darkness of the dungeon and depended upon it for concealment are compelled by the change to seek another habitation or adjust themselves to the new conditions. Because those creatures love the darkness and do not wish to be disturbed it is not a kindness to continue to maintain dungeons for them to exist in. Evolution says, "Move on or cease to cumber the earth with your presence, since much is still to be gained before the night comes on when all things must rest."

For example: Here is an optimist who is a tourist and has reached a resting place in the sunlight on a mountain above the shadows of the valley below. He looks back upon his fellow-travelers who are struggling and stumbling over the path which he has trod. And because he has travelled the same road he is in a position to direct and advise the others. But until they have completed the first part of their journey and have approached sufficiently near to see the point of vantage the optimist has reached, they can neither understand nor appreciate the value of any advice he could give. Because he knows that he and all his fellow-tourists are living in eternity now, he has ceased to worry or to hurry. He knows that the mountain he is climbing is one of the eternal hills, and will continue to be in the same place long after those who are now struggling up its rough and rocky sides have left this mundane sphere, and he stops and rests and enjoys the scenery. But to the man below him who has limited himself to a three months' vacation from business, and who thinks he must "get the worth of his money," by crowding as much sight-seeing as possible into those three short months, the deliberation of the optimist is positively aggravating. He feels that it should be resented by every active, industrious individual in the party, and remarks to the person nearest him that "life is too short to be spent mooning over clouds and colorings." He frets and fumes because some of the party are late for the first train back to the hotel, and he paces up and down the platform before the railroad station and works himself into chills and fever because he is obliged to wait for the next train. He missed seeing the glorious sunrise, because he was running after his courier to know if the lunch basket had been properly packed; and he did not see the sunset because he was mentally upset about missing his train.

The optimist knows how the pessimist feels, because, at one time, he felt the same about similar trifles; but he also knows better than to argue with or attempt to show him his mistake, because his interference would be resented. So he looks unmoved upon the tempestuous outbursts of temper and smiles while the pessimist storms.

When the three months' tour is ended and the party returns home, the pessimist has only complaints to make regarding his experiences. He went away with the anticipation of getting rest and pleasure, but instead found only disappointment and fatigue. His expenses were much more than he was able to bear, and he remembers nothing but the misfortunes and mishaps which befell him. He finds that everything at home and in his business has gone wrong during his absence. Burglars entered his house, as he knew they would, and took away his silver. At his place of business the cashier decamped with the contents of the safe, as he feared he would, and he himself is bitterly discouraged.

All this happened because his objective mind was in control of the situation and had rushed him around without an aim or a purpose. He wanted to go some place, but was not quite certain where. He did not go to the mountains to see the wonderful productions of nature, but because others, whose society he desired, were going. His objective mind caused such confusion that he could not hear the intuitive suggestions of his subjective mind, had they been made to him, and he was constantly getting into trouble because of his lack of intuition and poise.

The optimist enjoyed every moment of his journey and saw enough wonders of nature for his thoughts to live upon during the coming year; and he returned rested and refreshed and ready to resume his work. Because he expected to find his home and his business in harmonious conditions, he found them so. He did not have his pocket picked, neither did he lose his purse nor any of his baggage. This was because he ruled his objective mind under all circumstances.

It is the objective mind that creates the bad karma and builds all the misfortunes for man.[1] And so long as man permits his lower, animal mind to control his affairs he will not become karmaless and free from misfortune. In the operation of the law govern-

---

[1] The History and Power of Mind, pp. 72-77.

ing Demand and Supply the law works more rapidly with the optimist than with the pessimist, because the karmic obstacles in the path of the optimist have been largely removed or overcome, while the karmic obstacles for the pessimist are still in the way and delay the coming of his demonstrations. Then, too, the optimist has ceased to create new karmic obstacles for himself, because he controls his objective mind, while the pessimist is constantly creating new karma through the activity of his objective mind. And these karmic conditions not only affect the present life, but it also affects conditions of the next birth.

For example: Here are two brothers, both born in poverty. They commence life under unfavorable financial conditions, and because of this both are pessimistically inclined; but as the years go by, the views of one of the brothers begin to change. He finds that his affairs run more smoothly when he looks upon life philosophically. He knows nothing of Demand and Supply as a law, but unconsciously uses that law, and by so doing overcomes much of his past karmic accumulations and also saves himself from making much future bad karma.

His brother, however, becomes a confirmed pessimist, and passes out of life in that unfortunate mental condition. The optimistic brother lives to old age, and passes out of physical life comparatively happy because of the poise he gained and maintained during the latter part of his life. When these two egos incarnate again the pessimist is born into poverty and misfortune as the result of the mental creations he made during his last life, and the optimist is born this time into affluent circumstances. His family and friends are well-to-do, and, because of the poise he had gained during his last life, this time he is born with increased individuality and mental force. In this incarnation the opportunity is given to each of these egos to learn something of the science of life, and both undertake to demonstrate for themselves. The man who during his last life was a pessimist does not have his demands met as quickly as does the optimistic man, and he becomes discouraged and wonders why the law does not work as readily for him as for the other man.

Divine Law must work through instruments, and those most available surrounding the pessimistic soul, through which his demands would most likely be met, are persons who, like himself, are in straightened circumstances. This is due to the operation of the Law of Attraction. He and they were attracted together because they were of a common or a like rate of vibration. If he makes a demand for money—being surrounded by persons who have none and have no opportunities for getting any—it could not come to him so soon or so easily as if he were surrounded by those who had it and who could be used by the Law as instruments to meet his demands. The Law then must find other instruments who can be used in this man's behalf. This often causes delay, because there are so many adverse conditions to be met and overcome, and one of the greatest of these is the free will of the persons whom the Law must use.

God—Divine Mind—never coerces Its children to do anything nor to give anything. It gives free will, but makes suggestions. If men follow their impressions, which are often Gods' suggestions, then they are working as Divine Law's instruments. But if they do not follow their impressions, then they do not work with the Law but against it.

It is not difficult for the Law to meet the demand of the optimistic brother who is surrounded by persons who have plenty of money, because the instruments through which such demands can be met are available. And perhaps because of his past associations with them there are karmic debts which they owe to him, and which may now be paid through the operation of the Law of Demand and Supply. But in time the demands of both men will be met.

The third element in the Law of Success is the conservation of force. By force is meant not only the mental, but also physical force. Because without a strong physical body the mental powers have no material center through to operate. The conservation of mental energy requires that the greatest expenditure of force should be directed toward the attainment of the particular success selected, rather than that it should be diffused in an attempt to attain success along several lines simultaneously. In other words, a person should devote the greater part of the time given to concentration in concentrating upon that particular success which he most desires to attain.[1]

To conserve physical force the personal magnetism of an individual must be maintained. A waste of the magnetic force may be caused in two ways: first, by voluntary depletion through overwork in behalf of himself or of others, and, second, through vampirization.[2]

Demagnetization, produced by vampirization of the physical body until it is no longer of use to the ego as an instrument, is a hindrance from which thousands of persons are suffering at this point in the evolution of the race. And this condition exists with both sexes, and should be declared against by every progressive, thinking, striving soul who desires to be of benefit to his fellow-men. It is not the duty of an individual to submit to vampirization, or to permit another to retard him in his evolution in any other way. If his karmic connections seem to bind him to an unpleasant environment he should either live out the disagreeable conditions, so far as the material or physical connections are concerned, or get out of them by demanding to be released; but in any event he should reserve and maintain his rights as an ego to think and to study and to grow in spite of the opinions of another individual to the contrary. Vampirization produces demagnetization, and when a man's body is demagnetized he has been robbed of his mag-

---

[1] The History and Power of Mind, pp. 162-167.

[2] The History and Power of Mind, pp. 44-46.

netic force until the atoms composing his body have ceased to vibrate or to rotate, harmoniously.

Magnetic attraction in the physical body is caused by the polarization of atoms. But the law of attraction which controls polarization operates with equal force upon all the planes of being. There is a positive and a negative side to everything in the world, and a body has magnetic polarity when the positive sides of the atoms composing it, contact the negative sides of the atoms nearest them; and demagnetization is produced by the destruction of this relationship. In other words, when the endless atomic chains of a physical body and brain have been broken, as it were, by the positive side of some of the physical atoms contacting the positive sides of other physical atoms, then, instead of a harmonious condition existing between the blood, bones, muscles and nerves, there arises an imperfect circulation of the blood, a crumbling or brittleness of the bones, a cramping or withering of the muscles and a jangling or paralysis of the nerves. And all this suffering may be caused by the daily contact of one physical body with another which takes its magnetic force more rapidly and in greater quantities than it can be drawn again from the magnetic cosmic forces surrounding it.

There are individuals upon the material plane who exist solely by magnetic vampirization.[1] They do not depend upon nor draw their forces from the cosmic currents, but, human parasites as they are, they live

---

[1]The History and Power of Mind, pp. 129-130.

upon the magnetism of other individuals; and if it should come to pass that they were to be isolated from other human beings their bodies would wither and die from a lack of magnetic supply. Although constantly submerged in the great sea of cosmic, magnetic force, they cannot absorb magnetism from it, because the currents which compose it are too rapid and too vast for them. But they can and do fasten upon other individuals, and, like leeches, absorb through the tiny, positive part of themselves the personal magnetism of their victims. This is because the atoms composing the bodies of such individuals are more negative than positive. They are not poised, and therefore their atoms do not rotate regularly. As compared with cosmic objects, they are meteoric and have no fixed orbit or elliptical motion. As compared with so-called inanimate things upon the earth, they are topheavy like inverted church steeples or baseball bats. Because of the negativeness of their physical atoms the bodies of these individuals are loosely put together, and are easily disintegrated. Such persons are always in trouble, and are constantly meeting with mishaps and misfortunes. They ask advice of every one whom they meet, but rarely follow it when it is given. They are always looking for some person to help them, either financially or physically, but usually resent mental assistance because of their own preconceived opinions. They desire to know of all the seeming misfortunes of other persons, and take especial delight in listening to a trial by jury of a noted criminal. If a murder or a suicide has been committed they will go any distance and suffer almost any inconvenience to see the mutilated corpse—and the greater the mutilation the more pleasure they seem to derive from looking at it. If a horse is killed by a motor car they will stand for hours watching the dead carcass, and will struggle and fight with each other for the best positions from which to see it. They buy and read the most sensational papers, magazines and books on the market, and then insist upon relating or describing the grewsome things they have read or seen to every one who will listen to them. This morbid condition of mind is due to the attraction of like to like. Because these individuals are irregular both in their mental and physical vibrations, they are attracted to the unusual and irregular conditions in life; and if there is a railway collision or a steamboat boiler explosion they are usually among the killed or injured.

Among electricians they would be called dielectrics, because they are non-conductors of force. They receive but do not give force, and that which they receive does not seem appreciably to improve their general demagnetized negativeness. Evolutionistically they are like the crystallized salts of ammonia, and must be dissolved into a fluidic condition and be mixed with other ingredients before they will be of much value to humanity. And since every physical thing is the material expression of the mind that produced it, it is but a natural consequence that the minds or souls of these negative individuals must necessarily be left behind by the progressive egos on their evolutionary journey. And this is not a regrettable thing to contemplate, since they will not be lost, but will each be taken back again into the bosom of the Infinite to be brought forth during another Cosmic Day. The real, regrettable feature is the fact that progressive egos, those who are capable of reaching higher planes of consciousness before the Cosmic Night comes on, are permitting themselves to be retarded in growth while submitting to the vampirization of these nonentities. For the strong souls who are waiting for them, and are hoping and trying to make something out of them[1] are under the hallucination that it is their duty to bear these others' burdens, because they are too weak or too indolent to bear them for themselves. This is a fearful mistake. Now that the race has reached its majority, every ego must stand or fall by itself; and those who are able to press forward and attain should be warned of the danger they incur by needless delay.

For example: Here is a woman, who is a strong soul, but is wedded to a man diametrically opposed to her in nature. True it is that a karmic connection brought them together in this life, but it was karmic only so far as the physical, or sex union was concerned. The woman is most anxious to read and to study along the lines of advanced thought. She knows that she is capable of progressing, but her husband, who is a fretful, spiteful, negative invalid, will not

---

[1]Linked Lives, p. 141.

permit a book or a paper advocating advanced thought to be brought into the house. He knows nothing about evolution or progression, nor does he wish to. But he demands and receives the undivided attention of his wife, and is even jealous of her thoughts. He does not permit her to be alone for a moment, either night or day, but watches every expression of her face and contradicts every statement she makes. He is not happy either with or without her, because happiness is a condition of mind he knows nothing about. He nags, and scolds, and yet clings to her, and keeps his body and soul together by aid of the magnetism he takes from her. Because she is wedded to him, she believes it to be her wifely duty to sacrifice her life, if it should be necessary, for his good, and, because he does not wish her to read the books he does not like, she refrains from doing so. Because he will not be left for a moment alone, she devotes her entire time to him.

He vampirizes her body until it becomes so badly demagnetized that she cannot use it, and she is finally forced out of her vehicle without having gained in this life any of the knowledge or wisdom she craved. Thus this whole incarnation has been wasted, so far as soul progression is concerned, because of her yielding to the selfish, personal wishes of a nonentity. Mentally and physically enslaved, as she was, by her mistaken sense of duty, she heard nothing but her husband's pessimistic opinions; and because of his inharmonious vibrations, optimistically inclined indi-

viduals were not welcome visitors at her home. And
thus not only did this ego lose this incarnation, but,
because of the pessimistic thought creations among
which she lived for so many years, she will be drawn,
in her next life, into a most wretched environment.
She will then be born surrounded with poverty, sickness and gloom, and she will be over-shadowed from
infancy to womanhood, and perhaps to the end of that
life, with the fearful materialized creations that were
mentally created for her in this life, and which she
tacitly accepted.

The Law of Mental Attraction operates as regularly and as unerringly as does the law of gravity,
which is a part of it, and therefore every mind or soul
is a center of gravity for itself. Man is a little vortex or world, and becomes possessed of everything,
whether it be for good or ill, that he pictures in his
radius or aura. As the thought creations of Gods and
of men exist within the atmosphere or aura of the
earth, and through the operation of the law of physical
attraction or gravitation are magnetically drawn to
the earth, and are held upon the earth, so do the mental creations remain in the aura of a soul, or little
world, until they are materialized and possessed by
those who created them, or for whom they were created. For, like the creative Gods of the heavens who
materialized Divine Mind's pictures upon the earth,
so men can and do create for other men as well as for
themselves. And if those creations are accepted and
are not destroyed by mental repulsion, they will mate-

rialize and do the work that their nature compels them to do. And the magnetic attraction of the mind for whom they were created will hold to them as tenaciously, although only possessed of them by adoption, as the material creations of earth are held in their positions by the gravic force of the earth.

LECTURE NINE.

DEATH.

From the moment that the objective or animal mind was created upon the earth, it has never ceased to fear the transition called death. This is due to its intense desire for life, and to the fact that it is utterly oblivious of all its past states of consciousness, and is entirely unconscious of a continued state of existence upon any plane other than the material, for the seat of memory of past incarnations is the subjective mind. To the objective mind, physical form is life, and therefore it believes that to maintain life, material form must be preserved. Since its desire for life is greater than all its other desires, disintegration of form, for the animal or objective mind, is the greatest misfortune that can come to it. And until each subjective mind shall be able to impress upon its objective mind the truth that life is God, and therefore is eternal, and that its personal existence is not dependent upon physical form, human beings will continue to fear disintegration of form more than anything else in the world.

Believing, as men did, that immortality could be gained only through the preservation of the material form, and, because they desired to meet again those whom they had loved and had so mysteriously lost through "death," they used every available means to preserve intact the deserted physical bodies, with the hope and the belief that at some future time those same forms would be re-animated and be restored to the bereaved who were left behind. Therefore it was the objective mind's desire for perpetuity that caused men, of a more remote period than this, to have their own and their friends' physical bodies preserved after the egos had departed to other realms.

By some peoples it was thought that "death" was a form of suspended animation and that, by means of it, the life principle, or soul of man, was locked into his body, there to remain until some great Celestial Being should come to earth and should arouse and restore him to activity. To persons of this faith the destruction or loss of a physical body caused greater sorrow, if possible, than did "death"; since such a loss prevented the possibility of resurrection and of consequent immortality. There were other peoples who believed that the ego of man was not locked inside his body after "death," but was bound to it by fetters that permitted it to go but a few feet from the body. And the followers of this faith believed it to be a sacred duty to daily place food and drink at the head or feet of the corpse, or somewhere within its reach, in order that the life principle could consume them and thus be kept strong and able to use the body when the time should come for it to be restored to activity. To these persons the failure to provide food and drink for an excarnated ego was a greater crime than was murder, and was punishable with slow torture, such as starvation, or some fearful affliction which was believed to be equal to what the soul suffered in consequence of the culprit's neglect.

To the Occultist there is no "death," according to the common acceptance of the term. The condition called "death" is a complete demagnetization of the atoms composing a material form. Complete demagnetization of a form produces entire disintegration of that form, and since the atoms, of which a form is composed, are held together only by the magnetic attraction that exists between them, disintegration cannot become complete until all the magnetism has been withdrawn from the form which those atoms combined to compose. Therefore, a physical body cannot be properly called dead until it is entirely disintegrated; and any or all artificial means which may be used upon it to prevent it from disintegration, only retard demagnetization.

In lectures six and seven of this course, vibration, and magnetic attraction and repulsion of the atoms were discussed, to which the student is referred. In lecture eight demagnetization by vampirization was introduced, and will now be further discussed, since vampirization is usually the beginning of disintegration or "death."

Demagnetization of a physical body is produced by the constant expenditure of its magnetism in greater quantities than it is received, and this condition may be produced in various ways. On page 143, the manner in which magnetic power or force is generated and expressed was touched upon, but in connection with the subject it may be well to add that, since the generation of force, which is always magnetic, is wholly dependent upon the rotary motion of the atoms composing a center, and, since the expression, or giving of force, is dependent upon the elliptical motion of a center, then it is not difficult to understand why the physical body of a man or of a beast generates the most force when it is resting or sleeping. In other words, natural sleep, which is absolute rest to a physical body or center, is the greatest generator of magnetic force of any condition into which that body can enter; and therefore, in order to prevent an early "death," or the demagnetization of a physical body, the same number of hours should be given to sleep as are given to physical activity during each day, or twenty-four hour cycle.

Every thing that has form, whether so called inanimate or animate, is created subject to cyclic law; and, during the first half of its daily, weekly, monthly, or yearly cycles it possesses much more magnetic force than during the latter half of those cycles. This is due to the fact that magnetic force is constantly flowing and ebbing through material forms, whether they are suns, worlds, or men. And this flowing and ebbing of magnetic force may also be called action and reaction, magnetization and demagnetization, or life and "death."

When a world is created and has been given its
orbit, one half of the time it travels toward its sun
and the other half it travels away from it. When it is
going toward the sun it is becoming magnetized and
is then generating more force than it is giving. But
when it is going from the sun it is giving more magnetism than it is receiving; and all inhabited worlds
are alike in this respect. For example take the earth.
From the twenty-first day of December until the
twenty-first day of June of each year, she is being
magnetized; because at that time the greater part of
her surface is locked in snow and ice, the vegetation,
which vampirizes her magnetism, is resting and sleeping, while she is receiving magnetic force from the
sun in greater quantities than she is giving it to the
creatures that are living and depending upon her for
that force. This period is her flood tide. But from
the twenty-first day of June until the twenty-first day
of December this order of things is reversed and she
is then giving to her dependents more magnetism than
she is receiving; because she has then turned and is
going from the sun, which she in her turn vampirized.
And then, too, during that time vegetation and lower
animal life have awakened from the winter's period
of inactivity or rest, and are drawing from the earth
magnetic forces in order that they may express them.
And thus on the twenty-first day of June of each year
demagnetization of the earth by vampirization begins.
If she were to continue to recede from the sun indefi-
nitely, that demagnetization would finally become

"death," or disintegration; and she and every form which now exists upon and vampirizes her would cease to exist as form.

And, as conditions now are, the earth is gradually giving more magnetism than she receives, and the time will come when she must rest or disintegrate. This is because, as she grows older, her responsibilities increase instead of diminish; for, as men and beasts multiply in numbers, more demands are made upon her for their maintenance and her natural resources are consumed in greater quantities. Her vital fluids and gases are drawn out of her, and, through consumption, are changed into hydro-carbon vapors and aeriform matter and are left behind in space as she whirls rapidly through it in her orbit. Then, with each added year, she is robbed of more and more of her minerals which, when in their natural states, as strata, serve as repositories for the magnetic force she receives from the sun during her flood tides.

But in Cosmos the Divine Law provides periods of rest for Its worlds and suns, as It provides opportunities for rest for men and beasts who live upon the worlds. These cosmic rests are utilized by the planets to the full limit of time given to them, and, because of these rests, are their lives and their usefulness prolonged. In the life of a world there are seven great periods of inactivity, each of which lasts as long as do its periods of action, and in this manner each world is enabled to regain some of the magnetism of which it has been robbed. But it never fully regains all, for, if that were possible, it would continue, in the form in which it began to exist, until the end of the Cosmic Day in which it was created; and this would not be desirable, since, in order that evolution may not be limited or delayed by old forms, all forms must be made to give way to new when their period of usefulness is ended. To illustrate a rest in Cosmos, a few pages will be quoted from the diary of an advanced student of Occultism.

"My Master promised that to-day we should go and see a world that is about to enter into rest for many thousand years, and it is with most intense interest I awaited his coming. At midnight he arrived and in a few moments we were on our way. * * *

At a great distance we saw a stellar group—a cosmic community—which, independent of all others, seemed to have become a system of its own. A mass of molten cosmic matter formed a central sun or magnet for the system and was at least a thousand times as large, and, although not nearly so dense, yet weighed, I think, three hundred times as much as does our earth.

"That great orb was enveloped in clouds of vapor, which, at so great a distance, seemed to have been created by the humidity of its surrounding atmosphere coming in contact with the intense heat it generated. And those vapory clouds were in a constant and a tumultuous commotion. At times they seemed to be tossed about as if a great consciousness were playing at golf with them; and then they became piled high upon each other like mountains, while from the glowing orb behind we saw a rich golden light that illumined them as if by calcium flame. Sometimes they were suddenly torn apart, and, through the rifts, there streamed great sheets of fire, which gave to them the appearance of billows of rose-colored foam. Then again the rifts were closed and the whole mass assumed a dull grey color as though a cloud of smoke had passed between us and the scene.

"As we came nearer, it was most evident that the flaming mass of molten matter, or sun, was whirling through space with tremendous velocity, and was dragging after it by its powerful magnetic attraction five smaller globes or satellites; and those worlds when compared with their magnet appeared as fireflies beside an arc-light; yet the smallest of them was considerably larger than our earth. Approaching still nearer, we discovered that the satellite furtherest from its sun was undergoing great changes. Drawn, as it was, by an irresistible force, it continued to follow its orbit, but its rotary motion had almost ceased, and, like a great dead fish upon the sea, it floated in space and was drawn helplessly in the wake of the monster orb that still attracted and controlled it. From its appearance I concluded that it was the oldest of the five satellites, and my Master told me that it was closing the sixth great cycle or period in its evolution.

"When we entered the atmosphere of that globe we

found it stiflingly hot. Great copper-colored clouds
hung low in the sky and the light from its sun had
been turned into shade by them. Gazing through the
hazy dimness of the shadows, it seemed that the glowing orb that served as sun had refused to longer give
of its light and brightness to that world. For, through
that dense atmosphere which could not be penetrated
by a lesser light, the sun had the appearance of a
dark, crimson sea of clotted blood; and as we looked
about upon the shadows it seemed as if its moon and
the stars had also refused to shine upon that helpless
world, and that it was left to meet its fate in darkness.

" 'Why does not the sun shine here the same as it
shines upon the other planets in this group?' I asked
of my Master; and he replied:

" 'The sun has not ceased to shine, but this planet,
because of its inharmonious condition, has created
these shadows that lie between itself and the sun. Its
vibrations and the vibrations of these clouds have obscured the sun's light. It is in the same condition
with a man who has become over-wrought with work
or with play, and, if it were possible to use the word
in connection with a tired world, I would say this
planet is suffering from cosmic neurasthenia, and for
a time must go into absolute rest or become disintegrated.'

"At that moment, just beneath us, we saw a ruined
city on that strange globe and went down to examine
its condition. Round us everywhere were evidences

of destruction and dissolution. There were monstrous heaps of stone that were now but the remnants of once beautiful buildings. And there were also crushed and crumbling walls that had once enclosed huge structures of most magnificent and lofty proportions.

"A race of beings both wise and powerful must have had their homes upon that planet, since such huge blocks of granite could never have been lifted to their elevated positions without the aid of powerful machinery that had been devised and operated by the intuitive minds and muscular strength of men. And, once having been placed, they never could have been dislodged and tossed into such abandoned confusion except by a terrific convulsion of nature.

"Everywhere there seemed to be an ominous calm that, like a fearful mental depression, had settled upon that ruined city and all the land surrounding it. Not a breath of air was stirring, and the vegetation was as dried as if it were standing in a fiery furnace. The leaves from the once beautiful shade trees had fallen to the ground and were curled and seared almost beyond recognition as leaves. Lying in the cracked and hardened soil at the bottom of a fountain basin were the withered roots and stems of what had been a water lily plant. All indications pointed to the fact that for many, many days this intolerable heat had been gradually increasing until it had absorbed all the moisture and had taken the lives of all the creatures who had lived in that place. It was also evident that the men who had built that city had deserted it; but my Master said: 'Come, let us go to the mountains, which are at some distance beyond the city walls, and search for the people who lived here.'

"It was as he expected to find. In the valley, on the brink of what had been a broad river, there were thousands of lifeless human bodies. The adults were gigantic in size; the half-grown children were like our full-grown men and the infants were like our children of five or six years of age. They had all fled from their homes to escape death from the falling walls of their dwellings, but had met it there in that valley by suffocation and thirst. For the river bed was dry and the dead and decaying carcasses of fish and animals were lying in heaps upon the bottom where they had died fighting for the last drop of the precious liquid—water.

"While we were gazing at the scene of ruin and distress, we became conscious of a trembling of the ground. Then there was a sound as if an explosion had occurred in the direction of the ruined city. It was followed by another and then another; and then we heard a fearful roar which seemed to increase in volume with every second until it seemed to come from almost beneath our feet. Then there was a swaying of the leafless branches of the trees, and a heaving up and down of the blackened soil, and soon there appeared great wide fissures where the ruined city had stood. A cloud of fire and smoke and gaseous fumes burst forth, and as suddenly and seemingly as easily as a pebble could be cast into a stream of water the remnants of the ruined city sank from sight between the awful jaws of that quaking ground. There was nothing left to mark the place where it had stood except a few stones which had helped to compose its outer walls.

"This was the first earthquake I had ever witnessed and it impressed me very strongly. While I was thinking of the great necessity that must have existed to produce such a fearful catastrophe my Master said: 'A storm is coming,' and, looking upward at the sky I saw that the copper-colored clouds had changed to a leaden grey, and it had become so dark that an object one hundred feet away was but dimly discernible. Then a wind commenced to blow in spasmodic puffs and soon splashing rain drops pattered down upon the heated stones in the river bed. At last those dreadful vampire clouds were giving back to that suffering world the moisture of which they had been robbing it for weeks and months. But it had come too late. All life was extinct and not a creature was left alive to taste it and to be revived.

"Far up the valley I heard a sound as of rushing wind. It came down the river course and brought a deluge with it. A sheet of water like a huge white curtain swept past us and from the heated ground a cloud of steam rose like a fog. The soil, cracked and hot, could not absorb the vital fluid in such quantities, and the torrents, rushing down the mountain sides, were received into the river bed and went sweeping swiftly on. The temperature, too, had fallen from torrid heat almost to freezing cold, and still I saw no prospect of a diminution of the dreadful storm. And now the clouds were almost black with unshed rain and I understood that a cataclysm had begun. * * *

"More than sixty days passed by before my Master permitted me to visit again that suffering world in what had seemed to me to be its death agony of fever heat and drouth; and when we went again we found all things submerged—except the mountain tops— and there was a cold greater and more intense than anything I ever knew. The waters were frozen into a solid sea of ice, and there was not a creature who could live a moment upon that globe in that fearful frigid state. It was indeed a frozen corpse, and, wrapped in its mantle of ice and snow, which served as a burial shroud for all its latent forces, it had sunken into sleep not to wake again until the great cyclic law should call its forces forth on its resurrection day.

"As we were leaving the frozen world, my Master said: 'It is with worlds as it is with men; they live, revolving about their central suns until their material forces have been spent and they become physically demagnetized and unfit for further use. Then their time of rest comes on. The throbbing, pulsing life force becomes suspended, or is withdrawn, and their consciousness is changed from action to inaction. For action must be followed by reaction as surely as darkness follows day.' "

Like the Universe, cyclic law has always existed and is a fundamental principle underlying evolution.[1] Like life, it has always been and will forever continue to be. It commences its operations with an individual from the moment of the creation of that individual and applies to men and beasts as well as to worlds. Because the earth is controlled by cyclic law, all the creatures who depend upon the earth for their existence are influenced by the same cycles or periods of time that control the earth. The inhabitants of other planets are also subject to cyclic law, but because of the difference between the size of globes and the consequent difference in the size of the orbit of each the cyclic periods on the different planets differ in length.

For example: The earth makes her revolution around the sun in three hundred and sixty-five days and one-fourth of a day; and this length of time upon this earth is called a yearly cycle. But the planet Uranus, being almost fifteen times the size of the earth, has so great an orbit as to require eighty-four years and one week of our time to make its revolution about the sun. And because the cyclic periods on the planet Uranus are so much greater than are those of the earth, the creatures that inhabit Uranus, being governed by the cyclic law operating upon that

---

[1] The History and Power of Mind, pp. 94-97, 103-104, 163-164.

planet, also have longer cycles and live to a much greater age than do the creatures upon the earth.

It is a self-evident truth that the more magnetic force a form expends, as a natural consequence, the sooner it will become disintegrated. And this is as true of the microcosm as it is with the macrocosm. The individual who works or plays for eighteen hours out of each twenty-four expends much more magnetic force than does the individual who sleeps and draws back to himself his forces for twelve hours out of the twenty-four. As the earth has its flood and ebb tides, or the coming and going of its magnetic forces, so does every creature living upon her have its flood and ebb tides; and if man would become wise enough to work with the cyclic law instead of against it, he would save himself much suffering and prolong his life to a greater length than he does.

The moment a child is born his flood tide commences, which lasts fourteen days, and is followed by fourteen days of ebb tide. He has then entered a world that will supply him with all the magnetic force he needs to use, but not to waste. Feeling his abundance of force, as a child, he romps and plays and expends much of it in this manner, but sleeps so soundly and so long each night, that he draws back to himself during those rest periods, more force than he has expended. Thus he is in constant possession of a sufficient surplus of magnetism to enable his physical body to grow and to expand. This condition usually continues to exist until he has reached his majority, and then his body usually ceases to grow. Because of his increased responsibilities, he then begins to expend more magnetic force than he generates, or receives. This is due to the fact that he does not spend so much time in sleep as formerly, and, if he labors to live, perhaps he works for ten hours out of each twenty-four and then recreates or dissipates during the greater part of each night. If he is in possesion of wealth and social position perhaps he may be imbued with the thought that he must "go the pace" or be disgraced, and then he searches for new and untried avenues through which he may expend or waste his magnetism. It is true that he may be unconscious of the results of his wastefulness, and perhaps he does not know that disintegration or "death" commenced its work upon his body at the moment demagnetization began to exceed magnetization; but ignorance of the law does not excuse or exempt its offenders from consequences, and, after a few years of dissipation, he begins to call himself "old man" before he really feels the age that is so rapidly approaching as the result of his extravagances in the expenditure of force.

When starting his career of dissipation the young offender of the law thinks "old man" a complimentary title, and bestows it generously upon himself and upon all the "other boys" whom he wishes to flatter. This is because the title implies extended experience in dissipation, in which he takes great pride until the time comes when, as a result of his physical excesses and frequent declarations that he is an "old man," and after some unusual expenditure of force, he is really brought to feel the age he has been declaring for himself. Then he begins to wonder why he cannot do the things he once did, and why a little fun tires him now so much. If he knew that "death" had already commenced to claim his body for its own, and that with every over-exertion or dissipation he was shortening his span of life, he would change his mode of living, the nature of his amusements, and his declarations for old age.

To prevent disintegration or "death," and to prolong the existence of a physical body to one hundred or to one hundred and fifty years, men must make some radical changes in their modern mode of living. They must give more time to sleep and more thought to what they eat and drink. At least one-half of a man's time should be given to rest or to sleep and his food should never be other than simple and wholesome. Highly spiced, and therefore indigestible things should be abolished. Pepper and all condiments containing peppers and mustards should never be taken into the stomach; since none of these do any good, are neither nutritious nor satisfying to hunger, and serve only as irritants to the internal organs and intestines the same as they do when applied to the skin of the body. For his beverages man should drink nothing but pure water, either hot or cold, and the unfermented juices of fruits. The time given to labor, or to the necessary and direct expenditure of physical or magnetic force, should not exceed four or five hours of each day. He should learn to recognize and work with the cyclic law by never making extra or unnecessary exertions during his ebb tides and during the last six months of his yearly cycles. He should watch the expenditures of his magnetic force and never continue them until physical exhaustion or depletion comes upon him.

During the last half of his century he should save his magnetism by sleeping and resting more than during the first half. And if by reason of some illness or mishap there should be an extra demand made upon his physical strength he should immediately supply that deficiency with electricity. When his century cycle has ended and the flood tide of his new century commences to supply him with its new force, if he has taken the proper care of his physical body and has kept it in a condition to receive and to make use of the new force, he will enter upon his new cycle with much greater physical strength than he possessed during the first ten or fifteen years of his first century's ebb tide.

But over-exertion or an unnecessary expenditure of magnetic force, for any cause, is not the only means by which demagnetization or "death" may be hastened or produced. There is the element of vampirization which must also be taken into consideration; and this is a very great factor in the process of disintegration. As men and beasts vampirize the earth and take her magnetic forces, so men and beasts are vampirized by each other and by the elements. In lecture eight an illustration was given of a negative individual vampirizing and living upon the magnetism of another until his victim's forces were so greatly diminished as to make it impossible to hold her body when complete demagnetization or "death" ensued. The illustration was not that of an unusual condition, but is more common than otherwise. For, either consciously or unconsciously, the stronger individuals are constantly giving their magnetism to those weaker than themselves with whom they associate; and, whether it be a man or a beast that suffers from this kind of vampirization, the results are the same.

Unconscious of the law governing the exchange of magnetism, it has been a custom with some persons to provide feeble or aged individuals with animal pets which they could vampirize. If a child were suddenly to become "ailing," as indisposition was sometimes called, it was often provided with a healthy puppy with which it was permitted to sleep and to play in order that it should regain its health. And elderly persons who are fast losing their magnetism often insist upon being permitted to sleep with children or with younger persons in order that their magnetic forces should be restored again. But if aged persons are not permitted to prolong their physical lives by vampirizing the force of younger individuals during sleep, then it is a very noticeable fact that they were happiest, brightest and strongest when they were surrounded daily by children, or by younger persons. The man of eighty who seeks a wife always selects, if possible, a woman who is much younger than himself. And it is not an unheard of occurrence for a wealthy widow of sixty, or even of seventy-five years, to buy for herself a young husband of thirty. This is vampirization, and whether of a conscious or an unconscious nature, its results are the same.

There is another form of vampirization which is by the elements of nature. In the same manner that man on a beautiful spring day draws or absorbs from the atmosphere the electric or magnetic force he needs and feels strengthened thereby, so do the cold, cutting winds of a frosty day in winter take from him his magnetism. It is a popular fallacy with the people who live in a cold climate, that it is healthful to walk, or to ride, or to be exposed to the freezing air of winter. And because such exposure brings the blood to the cheeks, it is believed to be revivifying to the individuals who indulge in it. This is as much a mistaken belief as is that which makes a man take a plunge into a tub of cold water in order that he may be temporarily stimulated by bringing the blood to the surface of his body by violent friction after the plunge.

A sudden shock to the system is always harmful, instead of helpful, and serves to shorten instead of to lengthen the span of life. Cold indicates a lowered rate of vibration. Cold water is vibrating at a lower rate than is warm or hot water. Cold wintry air is vibrating at a lower rate than is warm spring air; and a warm body, if exposed to cold air, or to cold water long enough, will become demagnetized or frozen. When a body is frozen it is called dead; and this condition is produced by the vampirization of the cold air or cold water, in which it has been submerged. The man or woman who persists in being exposed to the cold winds of winter is voluntarily submitting to vampirization and is hastening old age and decrepitude. The physician who tells a person to bare his neck to the cold in order to become toughened to the cold, and promises health to that person in consequence of his exposure, is either ignorant of the law which operates as vibration, or he is looking for another patient. The woman who persists in exposing her face without a veil to protect her skin from the vampirizing cold air, becomes aged and wrinkled in appearance, and the muscles of her face grow weak and flabby in consequence of the exposure. A glance at the wrinkled and grizzled old sailor who faces the storms before the mast should be a sufficient object lesson to show her the results of exposure to cold air and cold water.

When the body and brain of a man are lowered below the normal rate his mental forces cannot manifest so well as when his blood is circulating and his body is vibrating normally, and this is illustrated by the different mental conditions of the different peoples on the earth. For example: The mind of the Eskimo is never so active as is the mind of an East

Indian. And history shows that the greatest civilizations have always been found in a warm climate.

But there comes a time when disintegration or "death" to the physical body or material form must come; and because of the breaking of family ties and of familiar associations this is often a sad occasion. To the evolving, developing ego who becomes disembodied, "death" is really a second birth into a higher realm or plant of consciousness, and it is through this transition that it becomes relieved of all physical pains and discomforts. But because of its love for the friends whom it is leaving, and who mourn and grieve because of its absence, it is sometimes made to suffer great mental depression and sadness and is thus prevented from entering fully into the joys of the mental and spiritual planes of being. This is because the sorrow and lamentations of its earthly friends attract and hold it to earth. By their wishing or demanding that it shall return to them, it is drawn back by the magnetic attraction of love, and it is sometimes deprived of mental or spiritual happiness for years because of the mourning of its friends.[1]

When the time has come for an ego to leave its earthly vehicle the real process of death is as natural as was the process of its birth into the world, and is not dissimilar. As the head of the human child is born first, and afterward its body, so the head of the ego emerges and rises above the physical head. Then slowly the shoulders and body appear, and finally its

---

[1] Linked Lives, pp. 198-199.

limbs and feet.   There are always disembodied egos
waiting to receive and assist the passing soul, and, if
the shock of its separation from the physical body has
been so great that it is unconscious for a time—as is
often the case—these disembodied friends support and
strengthen it until it has regained consciousness and
enough magnetic strength to support itself.

For the first few hours after its disembodiment an
ego is never so strong as afterward, because so much
of its magnetic force is still left in its deserted physical body.   But as the body grows cold, because of the
cont;nuous lowering of the rate of vibrations of the
atoms composing it, the magnetic force is drawn into
the ego who has just left it.   With this added magnetism the disembodied ego gains strength and greater
consciousness, and if the physical body should be cre-
mated, and not embalmed or entombed, the ego is liberated from its material body as soon as its physical
atoms are dispersed.   For there is a magnetic cord
that binds the ego to its body until complete disintegration has taken place, the same as the umbilical
cord unites the infant to its pre-natal envelope, and
it is as great a kindness to sever the magnetic cord
and liberate the ego by cremation, as it is to cut the
umbilical cord of the newly born infant and set it
free from its incumbrances.[1]

But sad as "death" or the disintegration of a physical body be to those who love and lose it, it is not to
be compared with the sadness which comes to the

---

[1]Linked Lives, pp. 195-197.

Beings who, by their missions, are sometimes compelled to witness the "second death" or the disintegration of another soul or ego. This is a dreadful fate, and it may be a small comfort to know that it comes to the minority instead of the majority of disembodied entities who pass to the subjective planes or realms. Diametrically opposed to the spiritual plane of consciousness called by the Eastern students of Occultism, Nirvana, is another plane which the same students call Avitchi. In our scriptures it is called Hell, and represents the very lowest depths of degradation into which an entity can fall. Not,iing but conscious, persistent and unceasing transgression of the Divine Law can bring a soul to this fearful place, a knowledge of the existence of which is never given to students until they are far enough advanced to be able to bear that knowledge without dangerously affecting them.

Further details concerning this state of consciousness will be given in the last lecture in connection with the subject "Homes of the Soul." It is sufficient at this point to say that "second death" happens oftener to objective or animal minds who, because of persistent wickedness, have been deserted by their subjective minds. But there are instances where a Son of God goes downward, instead of upward; where it continues to yield to the suggestions of its animal mind until it comes to a point where it deliberately and consciously chooses the left instead of the right

hand path, and then it goes down into the nether
world, instead of up into the higher, spiritual realms.

Second death is produced in much the same manner as physical death or disintegration. The vibrations of a dying soul grow slower and slower, and
its specific gravity grows denser and denser until it
can no longer remain upon what is called the first
subjective plane or purgatory, but is drawn by the
law of attraction, which is also gravic force, down to
a lower plane, to continue there its wretched existence
with others of its kind. When disintegration really
commences, like the old demagnetized physical body
it has left, it begins to grow dark and darker as its
density increases, until it becomes as black as the
realms into which it has descended; for there is not
one ray of light that penetrates the greatest depths
of the awful darkness of that place. Then the form
of the dying soul commences to change in shape.
First the legs and arms usually begin to diminish in
size and length until they have disappeared altogether, leaving the head and body. Then the body
commences to disintegrate and gradually disappears
until there is nothing left but the head with its distorted features. And thus this disintegration or second death continues for centuries.

But before the form of the dying soul begins to disintegrate or be dismembered there is always a hope
that it may be saved from that fearful fate and be
raised to a higher plane of consciousness. There are
strong and beautiful egos who voluntarily go down

into those dreadful depths to try to help and to save
the denizens of that nether world. If, as sometime
occurs, one half of a soul has gone wrong and has
sunken into hell while the other half has evolved to
a point of development where it is able to undertake
the work of trying to save its half from annihilation,
or "second death," then it descends and approaches
as near to it as its vibration will permit; and there
it whispers words of encouragement and consolation
to the sinful sufferer and offers help if it will but try
to rise again.

To an incarnated ego it would seem that any soul
who had sunken into that place would need only an
opportunity for escape to consent to liberation, but
such is not the case. In Avitchi or Hell a soul becomes so depressed with its wretchedness, so discouraged and so pessimistic that it often refuses to make
the least effort to change its mode of thinking; in
order to rise out of its condition. This is because, by
its many lives of perversity of thought and action, it
has brought itself into a mental condition which holds
it as firmly as prison walls and iron doors hold an
incarcerated prisoner of State.

It is a sad picture to see a beautiful ego pleading
with its unhappy half and attempting to raise or to
lead it to where it may catch a glimpse of a higher
and a better plane of consciousness which may be
gained if it will but make an effort for itself. No
soul has either the power or the right to save another
against its will; and it matters not how far it may

have advanced in its development, it cannot bring another into happiness without that other's co-operation and conscious effort in its own behalf.

Sometimes these unhappy beings are convinced and persuaded to retrace their steps and thus rise out of their wretchedness. But more often they will neither respond nor listen to those who would help them. Then they gradually sink lower and lower while becoming more and more wretched until at last complete disintegration or re-absorbment into the lowest or black cosmic current obliterates them forever from the Universe as individuals. And this is "second death." A most horrible picture to contemplate, but not so bad as the traditional one of souls burning forever and ever in a lake of fire and brimstone prepared for erring mankind by the devil and his angels.

LECTURE TEN.

AFTER DEATH.

When the indestructibility of the soul began to be accepted as a fact by the thoughtful people of the world, immediately thereafter there arose a most important question: "What becomes of the soul after death and after the human body or the material means of physical expression has been destroyed or disintegrated?"

To meet and to answer this question, from time to time, many theories have been offered to the world as truths by certain individuals who claimed to be holy men, and who were supposed to be inspired by God to teach Divine Law to others. But because a great number of their theories were both unreasonable and cruel, and differed so greatly in their characteristics from what man daily saw and knew of God and of His laws, after a time incredulity began to take the place of credence in regard to the teachers and their teachings. And, notwithstanding the fact that anathemas loud and deep have been sent forth from the so-called divine expounders of truth against all persons who have dared to think or to live contrary to the rules laid down by them, men and women have gone steadily on in their various ways and many have become independent thinkers.

In the beginning of the Christian era the followers of Christ began teaching and healing humanity, according to the manner in which the Nazarene had taught and healed before them. Later they decided, after many sad experiences, that it was necessary to teach something besides the doctrine of love to the cruel, animal men of their day. Instead, therefore, of following in the footsteps of the Nazarene and continuing to teach, as He had, that God is a loving Father and is ready to receive and to help all His children, they disgressed from the path of true Christianity and began to use hell and eternal damnation as a club to beat men into submission, and to force them to worship according to their dictates. And after the same manner that some parents believe it necessary to frighten their children into submission and obedience by promising to bring a "boogie man" to get them, the early Church fathers succeeded in frightening men into obedience and submission by threats of the devil and a future punishment. And when they found that men could be influenced through their fears more readily than through their loves, they intensified their frightful teachings by painting such pictures of a future state of existence, for those who did not accept the tenets of the Church, as would have made the heart of the loving Nazarene sad.

Believing, as many of the Church-father's did, that the Christian Church was the only door to salvation, and that every soul who did not enter it was doomed to destruction, they spared no pains, nor did they hesi-

tate to give their wildest flights of fancy for inspired
truths, which they believed would serve to bring
souls into that institution. And, since a story never
loses details by being continuously repeated, as the
years rolled by, the stories of hell, as given by the
early fathers, lost nothing by their constant repetition. When they saw how well their schemes had
worked toward increasing the membership and consequent support of their Church, they redoubled their
efforts and their falsehoods. After a time, forgetting
or ignoring the fact that the Nazarene had said:
"Suffer little children, and forbid them not, to come
unto Me; for of such is the kingdom of heaven," they
invented new hell horrors by including unbaptized
and stillborn infants with sinning adults on their
lists of candidates for that dreadful place.

But, like all other destructive things, by reason of
their own natures these deceptions finally returned
upon and destroyed themselves. The unreasonable-
ness and the injustice of such a thing as infant damnation finally arose like a grinning skull and horrible
cross bones between the faces of bereaved parents and
their God, until it came to pass that either God or
creed must go out of their hearts. To some persons
those teachings brought materialism. Many men and
women became infidels and repudiated God altogether. Others went insane over the grief and passed
out of life mentally unbalanced. Then there were a
few who were brave and strong enough to repudiate
the belief in hell and banded themselves together into

a society called Universalists, and declared that hell
was upon earth, and that man received his punishment as he went through life and not hereafter.

Anciently all teachers wore cowls and skirts, and
while thus attired demanded and received a reverence
from the people which greatly aided them in control-
ling their worshipers. This was because the teachers
so nearly resembled the pictures of the heavenly
saints whom they professed to represent upon earth.
But, gradually, as the more modern clergymen commenced to adopt a style of dress less saintly and more
fashionable, much of the halo of sanctity was removed from their personalities. It became quite difficult for the mass of men who had so blindly wor-
shiped signs and symbols, as interpreted by teachers
clad in vestments, to accept as Divine Truth anything,
given to them by men dressed in trousers and waist-
coats. And, notwithstanding the terrible threats of
eternal damnation so generously bestowed upon them,
many evolving souls revolted from the tyranny of the
Church and adopted newer and easier forms of worship.

This religious reaction was in perfect accord with
Divine Law, which always brings reaction to follow
action along any line of thinking or doing. It was
natural that there should be a relaxation from the
established forms of worship, even to the extent of
a disbelief in a future punishment, or even regarding
a future state of existence. It could not be otherwise
after the people's long submission to the ironclad

creeds and dogmas of a Church which depended for its corner-stone upon hell and damnation instead of Divine Love.

When mankind had reached a point where it really wanted to know the truth, there occasionally appeared an individual with intellectual strength and mental poise sufficient to enable him to rise and denounce all man-made creeds, and to declare that there is no anthropomorphic God, but that this is a universe of law, in which all men have the right to a freedom of thought and a freedom of speech. When first these intellectual giants appeared before the people and repudiated the teachings of the Church, the fear enslaved souls expected that God in His vengeance would pour out His wrath upon those men and that they would speedily meet with some terrible physical or mental affliction. But when it was seen that those heroes of the times were still permitted to live and to speak what they believed to be true, many, who had become surfeited with the old orthodox teachings and who really desired freedom of thought and action, accepted their words as expressed truth.

On January 29th, 1737, Thomas Paine was born. And during his life, which lasted about seventy-two years, he did more towards freeing the American people from their mental bondage than any other man previous to him. Such a storm he raised with his "Common Sense" and his "Rights of Man"—for which latter book he was outlawed from England—was never equalled until Robert Ingersoll stepped upon the lecture platform, and, striking his intellectual ax into the roots of that deadly nightshade of superstition, called "eternal hell fire," finished the work that Thomas Paine commenced almost a century before him.

Since 1876-1886, when Robert Ingersoll did his great work for the English speaking people of the world—who were privileged to hear his voice or read his lectures—a belief in hell and eternal damnation has steadily waned. Even the ministers of the gospel who at that time so frantically and fiercely denounced him as an agent of the devil and declared that he was robbing the Church of its most valuable and sacred tenet, have been compelled to modify their doctrines. And now, at the beginning of the Twentieth Century, fore-ordination, infant damnation and hell fire are seldom alluded to either in the pulpits of the civilized world or in polite society. For the churches have learned that they must keep pace with progression or fall out of the evolutionary race altogether.

Since dire future punishment for terrible crimes is no longer predicted, people have now become lulled into a false sense of security. They have swung to the other extreme and believe they have nothing to fear as punishment, except public opinion, which is sometimes very gently expressed concerning society's favorites. And because of this belief, a large portion of the human family has entered again into indulgences and transgressions against Divine Law which it dared not enter while bound by the fear of hell. The individuals who believed themselves to be God-fearing were mistaken; they were only hell-fearing, and now that hell has been wiped off the religious map they are neither the one nor the other.

The race has reached its majority, and is like the boy who has recently become a man. He can vote, and therefore is no longer obliged to submit to the autocratic rule of his parents. He is now too large to be chastised, and therefore threats have ceased to frighten him into submission; and yet he is not wise nor good enough to live up to the best that he knows. Because of the strictness of his past training and the watchfulness of his parents, he was not permitted to indulge in the excesses which he secretly desired. But now that all restrictions have been removed, he is satiating himself because he believes there will be no consequences. He is mistaken. There are and will be consequences, both here and hereafter, and although he may not meet with the devil of ancient theology and may not be plunged forever and forever into the lake which burns with unquenchable fire, still he is at a critical point in his evolution and cannot escape the results of his transgressions. It all depends upon how high he climbs or how low he sinks upon this material plane where his future state of existence will be. For in the Father's house there are many mansions, and a place is prepared for him which is best suited to his development. And there will be nothing but his own efforts which will change his condition.   In that other state of existence the wealth or social position which he enjoys here will have no power to help him.   He will then be recognized for just what he is.

Below this material plane and below the first subjective plane are the lowest conditions into which the egos of this earth can enter.   By the Eastern students of Occultism it is called Avitchi, and in its lowest depths it is indescribable in its horrors.   In its upper portion it vibrates red, while the lower vibrates black. It is the home for lost souls and egos or for those who have deliberately chosen to do evil instead of good. When, by reason of its thoughts and acts, a soul's vibrations have become more gross than are those of the earth, and, because of this condition, it is unable to longer resist the gravic attraction of the earth, through the operation of the same law that draws a stone to the bottom of the sea or to a point where it meets with obstructions as dense as itself, that unfortunate, misguided soul is drawn by gravic force lower and lower into obscuration and darkness.   Then it becomes disintegrated through vampirization by the black cosmic current in which it dwells.   The red cosmic current not only surrounds and penetrates the surface of the earth, but it also permeates it, becoming black towards its center.   Its darkest, deadliest shades are as destructive and as disintegrating to a dying soul and ego as corrosive acid is destructive to a material body.   It eats, consumes or absorbs the soul atom by atom until it is entirely disintegrated.

Let it be understood that souls and egos are not lost or destroyed through the vindictiveness of an angry God, but through their own willful sinning, and in no other way.

Notwithstanding all the book lore that has been given to man by the scientific investigators of material phenomena, he knows very little of what the earth contains beneath its surface. And the human race is almost as ignorant concerning the world it dwells in and of the subjective planes surrounding it as the blind mole in the meadow is unconscious of man's political and social relationships. If the human family were to be entirely limited to the few sodden crumbs of knowledge which are occasionally thrown to it by so-called scientific men, who believe in the existence of nothing that cannot be measured or weighed by their material rules or scales, then the school of evolution would necessarily be closed during the greater part of the time, and man would be unable to make much progress in his development.

But because there are advanced egos upon earth[1] who wish to know the truth, whether it squares with their preconceived notions or not, it is possible for those less advanced to profit by the results of their investigations and experiences, and a few pages will here be quoted from the diary of the same student of Occultism who so kindly contributed from his basket and store, for lectures Six and Nine.

"I have often asked my Master to show me the

---

[1] The History and Power of Mind, pp. 19, 20, 23, 26, 27, 64, 186.

abode for lost souls, and each time he had sadly refused, saying, 'You could not bear it now.' But to-
day, after being an accepted student for almost seven
years, he offered to take me into Avitchi as far as it
was possible for an incarnated soul to go. And when
I saw the horrors of that awful place, I ceased to
wonder why he had heretofore refused my request.
When liberated from my body and ready to descend
into the bowels of the earth, I was surprised to see
how easily an ego could penetrate dense matter. In
a vague way I had expected that my Master would
take me to some extinct volcano and use it as a pass-
ageway to the lower realms; but this was not the
case. Before we had descended to any considerable
depth he took me by the hand and said, 'Whatever
happens, do not let go of me, since an inexperienced
ego, if left by itself, is sometimes caught between two
entities—denizens of the lower plane—and is de-
tained and demagnetized by vampirization until the
magnetic cord between the physical body and their
victim becomes absorbed, and dissolution of the physical body necessarily ensues,' and, thus warned, I
kept close to my Master, and it was well for me that
I did.

"After descending for several hundred feet into the
earth we first came to a number of caverns which
opened into each other. There was a subterranean
stream of water that poured forth from a great hole
in the rocky wall and flowed through the place from
end to end and disappeared with a roar over the edge

of a yawning abyss in the last cavern. The walls of this place were glistening with minerals, and there were veins of ore among those rocks that would have driven a miner insane with greed. At the bottom of the shallow stream there were great quantities of gold that, by the constant washing of the swiftly running water, had been cleansed from earthy deposits until it glittered and shone most tantalizingly.

"At first I was so intently interested in those rocky caverns and our surroundings that I had not noticed that for a distance around us of ten feet or more there shone a strange blue light, which made the walls and floors glisten with a weird brilliancy. But when the thought occurred to me that the light from neither sun nor moon could penetrate to this depth without an opening in the earth, I began to wonder where the light came from, and, turning to my Master for an answer, I saw that it emanated from him.[1] In this darkness he had become a luminous body and was lighting the place with his brilliance. In reply to my mental query he smilingly said: 'Egos, like other things, always shine by contrast with unpleasant surroundings, and we must have light upon the subject that we are studying.' And then I knew that his modesty forbade him from saying that he possessed the power, at any time or place, to create light, according to his will. Forgetting everything except his wondrous power, I stood gazing admiringly at him until, wishing to divert my attention from him-

---

[1] Mata the Magician, pp. 12, 16, 20, 21.

self, he said: 'Look yonder,' and looking in the direction he indicated, I saw a group of entities who were watching us.

"Standing as they did among the shadows, that appeared the denser by contrast with the light that encircled us, they looked more like apes than men. With distorted features, grinning mouths and bulging eyeballs, they made a wretched picture to look upon, and I shuddered as I gazed. They all appeared to be startled, half blinded and disturbed by the light that had come so suddenly into their abode, and they huddled together, as if afraid we would attack them. Taking my hand, my Master led me forward until we were near enough to let the light shine full upon the group, and thus I had the opportunity to see each one very plainly. Had their figures been straight and erect, I should judge that they had been men who measured six feet while in physical life; but now they were bowed and bent and had huge humps between their shoulders. Their legs were crooked and withered, their arms were covered with knots or bunches, and their hands and fingers looked like claws, while their feet resembled the feet of bears.

" 'Do you know who these individuals were in life?' I asked my Master, and he replied: 'They were members of the Spanish Inquisition and have no subjective minds, since those left them long before they excarnated. These are now animal souls or objective minds, which were too strong for their subjective minds to control and have been deserted and left to their fate.[1] When first they passed from physical life they lingered for a time in Purgatory or upon the first subjective plane of being, casting their diabolical influence upon the minds of such men as they could control, until, weakened by their unwise expenditure of magnetic force, and thus losing their power, they were swept from the first plane by the law of evolution or adjustment, which soon places every individual where it belongs.[2] By reason of their density, these entities settled here, and will remain in this place or condition until there shall be another cyclic change or movement of the law. Then they will descend still lower, since, being only objective minds, there is no hope of their ever being raised from this condition.'

" 'Will you tell me something about the operation of the cyclic law you have just referred to?' I asked.

" 'During the latter part of the ebb tide of each century, as men now reckon time, there comes a readjustment upon all the subjective planes of being surrounding and interpenetrating the earth. Egos who are progressive are permitted to reincarnate, but those who will not progress, and who have karma to expiate, are compelled to reincarnate or to move downward. If for lack of strength or for karmic reasons a soul is unable to reincarnate and is on the downward instead of the upward course, then it is swept off the plane where it has been functioning,

---

[1] The History and Power of Mind, pp. 170, 171, 176, 177.

[2] The History and Power of Mind, pp. 109-111.

and, by gravic attraction, settles into a lower condition or state of consciousness; and thus it goes gradually downward until final disintegration or reabsorbment into the lowest shade of the black cosmic current becomes its fate. Shall we pass on and examine the next lower condition?' he asked, and again we started forth on our tour of investigation.

"It is a wonderful earth on which we live, and until I had the opportunity to study it by the light of soul, I had no idea of its almost limitless resources. There are vast beds of coal and great wealth of minerals, and there are rivers and lakes of petroleum which have never yet been touched by the probing iron tubes that men are so constantly sending after them. There are underground rivers and lakes of water and caverns so great that our largest buildings would seem like children's playhouses if they were to be put into them. As we swiftly passed from wonder to wonder, we saw many unfortunate beings who had neglected their opportunities for progression and were now taking the consequences. Some looked frightened, others sad and despairing, but many were rebellious and bitter. They were of many shades of darkness and had now nothing to do but to meditate upon their mistakes or to dispute or quarrel among themselves. As we passed or paused to look at them they usually returned our gaze; sometimes stupidly or wonderingly, but more often apprehensively, since the fear of greater calamities seemed to prevail with each. They never spoke to us unless we addressed them first, and this we did not care to do except in one instance, when we found a creature who had been a woman during its last incarnation and still retained something of what I imagined was her former appearance. She had been a Voodoo sorceress, my Master said, and was really a subjective and objective mind gone wrong together. This ego had deliberately chosen to do evil instead of good, and was suffering the consequences of its choice. It was surrounded by a number of other entities, who had been her victims in times past, whom she had been instrumental in helping downward instead of upward. When we came into the presence of this creature it rushed forward with outstretched arms as if it were about to seize us. But, stretching out his hand and giving it a look which seemed to have the power to stop a whirlwind, my Master spoke the one word, 'Stop!' and immediately it fell upon its knees as quickly as if it had been knocked down with a club. Then with his hand still raised, and, without taking his eyes from the creature's face, he said: 'If you have anything to say you must say it where you are. You cannot come any nearer.'

" 'Help! help! help!' it shouted in a tragic tone of voice, 'I want to get out of here!' and it commenced wringing its hands and swaying its body backward and forward while its eyes gleamed wickedly.

" 'What would you do if you were to be helped out of your condition?' Master asked.

" 'I would kill the man who murdered and sent me here,' it replied viciously. 'I would search the world

over, and when I found him I would strangle him
with my hands as he strangled me; and then I would
drag him down to my own condition! Will you help
me to get revenge?' it suddenly inquired, looking at
Master with its reddened eyes that blinked and
squinted under the radiant light that surrounded us.

" 'Not while your only purpose for release is revenge,' he replied, and, as we turned away, it sent
after us such curses as made me shudder at their
wickedness.

"After spending considerable time in looking about,
my Master said: 'Now that you have seen so many
phases of this wretchedness I shall show you the place
which first gave rise to the Bible legend of hell or of
the lake which is supposed to burn forever and forever
with unquenchable fire; for that, like nearly all those
old legends, was founded upon fragments of truth.'

After passing under many miles of sea and then
down deep into what seemed to be almost the center
of the earth, we came into the greatest of all the caverns I had seen. It was so immense that I was impressed with the thought that we had really entered
another world until my Master said: 'This is hell.
Into greater depths than this we cannot go; but I
am told that there is a place even worse than this
where all forms become slowly absorbed except their
heads, which remain conscious and which continue to
float about upon a black sea of cosmic consciousness
like corks upon the surface of a stream. And finally
after many centuries, the heads, too, become absorbed

and are drawn back to help swell that great torrent of destructive cosmic force, the upper portion of which is red and is constantly sweeping round and through the earth; and which is ever ready to supply animal man with material for his passions and his lower emotions."[1]

"This great cavern which we had entered seemed to be a center of attraction toward which much of the vital fluids and gases of the earth were drawn. There were monstrous holes in the walls and roof that looked as if they had at some time been vents and had served as chimneys to the place. And everywhere were heaps of rocks that looked as if they had some time been heated and tossed about like great balls of putty by some tremendous force, and had then been left to harden into their present grotesque shapes. There were also deep, dark pools of water and streams which gushed or trickled according to their size or volume from among the rocks and crevices. Here and there we saw hiding and dodging among the shadows the ugly misshapen forms of some of the denizens of that place. Going further into the cavern we found that, after the distance of a mile or two, the floors began a gradual descent, and the further we went the sharper became the decline until we seemed to be going downward at an angle of about forty-five degrees. And still on every hand, before and behind us, were heaps and piles of rocks which we passed over, through or between upon our journey. After a time

---

[1]The History and Power of Mind, pp. 135, 136, 140, 142, 143, 224, 230.

from out the shadows and the darkness there came a
glimmer of light in the distance, and I paused and
asked my Master what was its cause and from whence
it came. He replied:

"'That light is from the fiery lake of which you
have been told. It is a burning pool. We are now
directly beneath the Island of Java, which is a vol-
canic formation upon the surface of the earth, and
which contains numerous craters which serve as vents
or chimneys for this lake of fire,' and on approaching
nearer I looked upon a scene that neither time nor
eternity will ever be able to obliterate from my memory.

"Below us at a distance perhaps of one thousand
feet was what seemed to be a huge caldron of liquid
rock. It was seething and bubbling and spurting
high toward the roof of the cavern as if it were being
forced upward by numerous fountains. And there
was also a constant and a terrific rumbling and roaring sound, and a trembling of the rocks around us
as if they were being shaken from their resting places
and were about to go plunging down the decline to be
melted again into lava in that fiery furnace. It was
impossible for me to estimate the area covered by that
boiling mass, since it was in such a constant and
tumultuous commotion that I could see but a small
portion of it. But as I watched it roll and heard it
thunder, and saw it swirl and dash about in its seeming efforts to consume everything within its reach,
and, as I became conscious of the sickening stench

that arose from its gaseous and sulphurous fumes, I understood why the theologians' hell had been so graphically described. Turning to my Master I asked: 'Am I to understand that this place was expressly prepared for lost souls?' and he replied:

" 'No. This condition is but the result of a meeting at this point within the earth of such of her fluids and gases as are combustible by coming into contact. The combination of sulphur, gases and oils with the different chemicals which are here in great quantities has produced combustion, and the continuous flow of oil and of gas into this center supplies the fuel that keeps it burning. This is the largest of the several lakes that now exist within the earth and which supply the different volcanoes with their fires.'

"At that moment I saw a group of entities approaching. Their bodies were coal black and glittered in the firelight as though they were covered with scales. All were deformed. Some had huge heads and broad shoulders, while their legs and arms seemed like slender sticks. Others had large bodies and small heads and eyes that looked like living coals of fire. All had monstrous mouths and huge ears, and as they approached I was conscious of a great fear. For of all the hideous creatures I had ever seen in all our wanderings, these were the worst. Drawing nearer to my Master, I said: 'Keep them away, for I am afraid,' and he replied: 'Be calm. For if you cannot command yourself then you cannot command them,' then raising his hand as he had done before to the voodoo sorceress he said: 'Stop!' You can come no nearer,' and immediately the creatures paused, hesitated, and then turned and went another way. At that moment I felt a change coming over me. I seemed to lose my poise completely, and I said: 'Let us go. I cannot bear any more of this,' and Master quickly took me out of that awful place.

"When next I had an opportunity to talk with Master I asked him why theological teachers had taught that the only place of future punishment was that lake of fire when there were so many other unhappy conditions. And he replied: 'Ancient teachers knew the truth, since many were clairvoyant, and were conscious of all the states and grades of happiness or degradation into which souls can come. But because that is the lowest extreme of an abnormal condition of which they were conscious they used it to frighten men into good behaviour. It was not prepared for lost souls and egos, but they sank into it by reason of their sinning, and by the same law of attraction egos may rise by reason of their goodness and wisdom to great spiritual heights.

*   *   *   *   *   *   *

"Since I have been seeing faces and forms and have been hearing voices, I have wished to go into Purgatory or upon the first subjective plane and see the egos as they appear in their different states of consciousness. But it was not until to-day that Master consented to show me about, always having refused before this with the remark that I was not prepared to meet either the dwellers upon the threshold or the egos of higher realms because of my emotional nature, which I did not yet control properly. But to-day, after severely testing me, he consented to make the attempt, but promised to cut our investigations short if I should lose my poise again as I did in Avitchi.

"At first it seemed incredible that there could be such throngs and crowds of beings upon the first subjective plane while incarnated souls were moving about among them utterly unconscious of their existence.[1] When first I was liberated from my body and took my Master's hand, it seemed as if it must be fête day and that every one was out upon a dress parade. For there were thousands who jostled and pushed each other about, played pranks or disputed and quarreled as men do at a country fair or when a circus has come to a country town. And there were the souls of animals running about and following both incarnated and excarnated beings and each other and seemed to be as tangible as were those whom they were following. There were huge dogs and small dogs, kittens, cats and rats. And there were monkeys that had been some one's pets, and who were as active in that parade as any other creature.

"In the country before we reached the city I saw the souls of cows and of horses and of sheep mingling with the incarnated herds or flocks of their kind, and it seemed that the first subjective plane was as greatly crowded with the souls of animals as with human

---

[1] The History and Power of Mind, pp. 174-175.

souls.[1] In passing through the fields I observed that the female animals were the greatest centers of attraction for the disembodied animal souls of their kind; and when I asked the cause of this my Master said it was because of the possibility of rebirth or reincarnation for the animals who were being drawn again into physical life. They were attracted to the female animals more than to the males because it was through them, as mothers, that they would again be able to gain physical expression. And what was true with the animals was also true with human beings. Some women, and especially those who were at an age and in a condition where motherhood was possible, were surrounded by disembodied egos who were ready for rebirth.

"Something that impressed me very forcefully was the fact that although we were walking upon the earth the same as if we were in our physical bodies, still the atmosphere seemed to have entirely changed in some places. We were not conscious of the heat, although it had been exceedingly warm before leaving my physical body. The sun was then shining fiercely and there was not a cloud to be seen in the sky. But now, in this new condition, the sun was obscured in the city which my Master wished me to see subjectively, and there were shadows so dense in some portions of it that it seemed as if twilight had fallen. And this was especially true in the lower quarters of the city, where gambling and prostitution prevailed. And

[1]The History and Power of Mind, p. 174.

when I asked why this darkened condition existed my Master replied. 'This is a mental atmosphere that is vibrating at a rate which you are conscious of as shadows. When incarnated men and women constantly transgress against truth, purity and honesty they create mental cesspools or vortices of gross vibrations which draw into them, by their attracting power, such disembodied entities or souls as are vibrating in mental accord with those who created such vortices.[1] It is not alone true that the doers of evil prefer darkness rather than light, but they also create darkness by the density of their thought vibrations. They establish clouds between themselves and the sun in the same manner that they establish barriers between themselves and the purer egos who dwell on the planes above them. Look there, for instance,' and he pointed to a large fine building which appeared to be an aristocratic family residence.

"Taking me by the hand, we entered the house without opening the front door, which was firmly bolted inside, and the bolts held in their places by strong steel chains. In the parlor we saw women who were painted like dolls and who were only half dressed, or were in evening costumes which made but poor pretence of concealing their voluptuous forms. They were lolling about on couches and easy chairs, while small tables, on which were bottles of liquor and finely cut wine glasses, stood just within reach of each. Behind, before and on either side of every

---

[1]The History and Power of Mind, p. 176.

woman in that room stood the disembodied souls of persons of both sexes who had been as low or worse than they in development. For there were women in that place who had been pure and true only a few years before, but who had strayed from the path of virtue, had yielded to a tempter in human form and had finally reached this condition. They were now never free from the effect that intoxicants have upon the physical brain, and because of this were much more easily influenced by the disembodied entities who were mentally urging them to drink and to sin. With a feeling of indignation at the condition into which these women had been enticed I turned to Master and said:

" 'Why cannot these women be made to see and know of the danger they are in? And why are they permitted to go blindly on to such a terrible fate as awaits them?'

"He calmly replied: 'If you do not control your emotion of sympathy better than this, I shall take you back to your body and you will not be permitted to extend your investigations for some time. These women are passing through this phase of experience because at present they have neither the desire nor the will to escape it. If you will observe you will see that the objective mind of each is in complete control of her actions. If I were suddenly to lift the veil and show them the entities who stand at their elbows, and if they were to be made conscious of the dangers they are approaching, they would scream and faint; and when they would return to consciousness upon the material plane, they would overlook the lesson which I had attempted to teach and would believe they had been the victims of a nightmare or of a joke. Then they would only drink the deeper to drown the fearful recollection. No. It is impossible to help a soul until it is ready and desires to be helped, for only then it will co-operate with its helper, and even then one must be wise enough not to do too much at one time, since none can bear more truth than can be immediately digested and applied to present conditions.'

"Passing on to another apartment on that same floor we found the man and woman who owned the house. They were sitting at a table and were playing cards with two other persons. It was not difficult to see that these two also were much further along on the downward road than were any of the women in the parlor. These, also, were drinking intoxicants and were using the worst language I had ever heard. They were gambling and also plotting against the fortunes and the lives of several persons; and, crowding around them so closely that they could scarcely be distinguished apart, were disembodied souls who were almost as dark and as devilish looking as were some of those whom we had seen in Avitchi. These entities mentally suggested diabolical plans to these human plotters and then laughed heartily when their suggestions were accepted.

"Rising to the floor above we entered a large, luxuriously furnished room where there was a young girl.

She was very handsome but most unhappy. There were glasses and liquor upon a table which she had not touched. When we entered she was pacing the floor and was wringing her hands in an agony of grief; and immediately my sympathies began to go out to her. But Master touched my hand and said: 'Remember your poise. If you lose it you cannot be of service to her nor to any one else whom you will meet. Now listen.'

" 'Oh, my God, my God, have you forsaken me?' she moaned. 'Why did I yield to that awful temptation! I must get away from this place and go back to my father. I will get out. I will, I will!' and she rushed toward the door just as a dissolute looking man stepped into the room. At sight of him the girl stopped, hesitated and finally sank into a chair. It was evident that he was the direct cause of her misery. Coming forward he smilingly made a flattering remark, to which she did not reply, but continued to look steadily and sullenly straight before her. At this moment Master stepped close to her side, and, pushing away the evil entities who stood around her and were mentally urging her into a passion, he whispered: 'You are repentant, not rebellious; and you desire to be good. You can and you shall escape from this place before you are compelled to sin again,' and these words he repeated over and over again to her.

"Sensitive to thought as the girl was, she seemed to listen to Master's suggestions, and immediately gained control of her anger. And when the man who had just entered laid his hand upon her shoulder caressingly, she rose and confronted him; and while the tears shone in her eyes, she said: 'You say you love me, and it was because of your protestations of love that I disobeyed my good old father and fled with you. You promised to marry me, but you did not do it. Will you release me and give me the money to return to my father?'

"At first the man looked surprised and then provoked and finally replied: 'Still harping on that subject which I thought you had forgotten. Why can't you be satisfied as you are? Haven't you everything a girl could possibly want?'

" 'No. I want my freedom from this den of iniquity. I want to breathe the pure air and see the sunshine again. I am sorry for my wilfulness and for my disobedience and wish to return home,' she replied sadly.

" 'But you are disgraced. Who will recognize you in the town where you were born and shone with such brilliancy for so short a time?' he sneered.

" 'My father will receive me and God will forgive me, and I don't care for the others. I want to be good and be happy again before I die,' she sobbed.

"Here Master stepped close to the man and whispered: 'Pity and release her; she is too good to live this life,' and this he repeated several times until the man received the thought and said:

" 'When would you like to go?'

" 'Now! this instant,' she replied, and started toward the closet for her wraps.

" 'But how can you pack all your gowns and get away to-day? Better stay another night,' he said slowly.

" 'I don't want ever to see those things again,' she replied passionately, 'for they would only remind me of my miserable mistakes, which I wish to forget. Please let me go now.'

"At that moment an evil entity came close to the man and was about to suggest something to him when Master stepped between the two and said: 'As you will some time hope for mercy, have mercy now for this girl,' and he suggested the thought with such force that the man turned pale and began trembling. After a moment he said: 'And so you shall go home, and have all the money that you will need to take you there. If your father refuses to take you back, let me know, and I will send you enough more to keep you honest until you can turn yourself somehow,' and handing her a large package of bank notes he said: 'Come, I will see you to the station,' and they walked together out of the house. Then Master said: 'She is the only person in this place who is ready to be helped, and now let us go.'

"The next place we visited was an opium den; down a narrow street into a Chinese shop where there were Oriental wares for sale. Finally we entered a large room in the basement of the building where the deadly drug was smoked. Here were men and women lying around the room upon luxurious couches that were piled high with silken pillows. These persons were in all states of stupefaction, and like the place that we had just left this, too, was crowded with disembodied entities in their different stages of undevelopment. All these entities had been opium smokers during their past incarnations, but now, not being possessed of physical bodies, could only enjoy their favorite indulgence by proxy—as the disembodied soul of a drunkard enjoys the fumes of intoxicants through vampirizing an embodied drunkard. These entities were nearly all objective, animal minds who had been deserted by their subjective minds, but were still strong enough to influence and to suggest the thought to their victims to smoke opium. When their victims had become completely stupefied and unconscious those vampires settled down upon them like huge black bats and, lying out at full length upon the prostrate physical forms, drew from them their magnetic forces until, after regaining consciousness, they could scarcely stand or walk. In this manner the vampires were able to enjoy the fumes of the burning opium and at the same time gain the magnetic strength they desired and needed in order to continue with their diabolical work.

"In this place there seemed to be no one who could be helped, since those who had been deserted by their higher or subjective minds were simply animal or objective minds incarnated in weakened and diseased physical bodies and were beyond help. And those who still were blest with subjective minds were not controlled by them, but were entirely dominated by their animal natures.

"As we passed through the city we paused for a few moments in many homes of the rich and also the poor, and saw much suffering, but some happiness in both. In every class there were individuals who were positively good and were living up to their highest ideals. The homes of these were filled with bright and uplifting vibrations and around such incarnated souls were disembodied entities who were suggesting beautiful thoughts to assist them in their work for themselves and for others[1] In other homes, often where there was much wealth and social honor, there was degeneracy and drunkenness. And this condition applied equally as well to each of the two extremes of society. Persons who had nothing to do, and those who would do nothing, were surrounded by disembodied entities of a like or of a worse nature than themselves, who suggested demoralizing thoughts which were accepted and acted upon. And nearly all these disembodied entities were earth-bound and could not pass to higher planes than the first subjective, because their love for material things was greater than for spiritual qualities. They stayed with the sensual because they loved sensuality; and would eventually either reincarnate or sink lower because of their grossness.

"Among the middle classes, with persons who were neither rich nor poor, but who were kept busy at work

---

[1]The History and Power of Mind, p. 186.

earning a living we found much greater mental development and more purity and truth. And I was strongly impressed with the thought that physical and mental activity are great protections against degeneracy and all kinds of sin. This is because the objective minds gain the greatest strength and power when their physical bodies are idle.

"After we had studied the first subjective plane, as it appeared in the largest city in our country, my Master said, 'I shall now show you something of the second subjective plane or first heaven which surrounds the earth outside the first plane. This is the temporary abode for disembodied egos who have struggled through and have overcome many of the temptations of earth; and have gained a point of development where they desire to progress instead of retrogress. For such, this is a resting place between earth lives where they may digest, as it were, their late experiences and assimilate the good that is to be gotten from each. When an ego has reached the second subjective plane, it is not likely, although not impossible, to fall into Avitchi. But if such a fate should befall it, then it is due to the fact that it was more negatively than positively good, and fell through lack of strength to resist some great temptation upon earth. After such an ego has been permitted to suffer for a time the consequences of its mistakes, usually a stronger one goes down and attempts to encourage and to assist it out of its unhappy condition. And that angel of mercy is usually the other half of itself.

But instances like these are rare, although they do sometimes occur.'

"It seemed as if a burden of lead had been lifted from my shoulders when we entered the atmosphere of that next higher plane; for we had indeed passed through purgatory and had at last entered a heaven of rest. There were no shadowy places, no darkness nor any gloom there. But there were trees and flowers and mossy banks and flowering shrubs. There were also beautiful places of abode and large magnificent buildings like amphitheatres, erected for assembly halls. And everything seemed to be as tangible and as firm to me as the earth had seemd to be to my physical body. In a vague way I had expected to find this plane a vapory, cloudy place, and I think I had even expected to find the egos who dwelt there transparent and intangible.

"A silvery light that reminded me of intensified moonlight shone everywhere. And there was a restfulness in the atmosphere of which I had never before dreamed. 'Let us sit here upon the bank of this stream among these flowers,' I said, and my Master consented. After the horrible scenes that I had so recently looked upon on the lower plane of being, this place seemed to be the height of beauty and bliss, and I said: 'Surely no soul could ask for more happiness than this,' and Master replied:

" 'This is indeed beautiful and restful, but there are planes beyond this where there are glories greater than these.'

"At that moment we saw two egos approaching, and as I gazed at them in speechless wonderment, my Master said that they were re-united half souls who were enjoying this paradise together after an earthly incarnation of suffering. Radiant with happiness they were the most beautiful beings I had yet seen, and, as they came nearer, I felt some of the love they radiated. Pausing at a short distance they smiled and waved their hands as if to welcome us to their heaven and then passed on. After resting for a time Master said: 'Come, you have kept your poise so well through these experiences that I shall now show you the next higher plane of being,' and rising, we passed on through gardens and groves, through fields and over hills, for what seemed to be a great distance. And during each moment I felt so uplifted and so happy that I hardly recognized myself in this new environment. On our way we met many beautiful egos, each of whom kindly saluted us, but did not offer to engage in conversation. Unlike mortals they appeared to be devoid of curiosity, although they must have known that I did not belong in their realm. As we were passing a large assembly hall, we paused to listen to the music, and what I heard in that beautiful place made a lasting impression upon my mind. Lover of music as I had always been, I had studied with the best masters available upon earth, but when I listened to the music on that plane I felt that never again should I wish to hear my own or another human voice lifted in song. The melody was so entrancing that I stood spellbound until it ceased, and then Master said: 'Come, we have but little more time. You have been away from your body longer than I intended and we must hasten back. But before we go, look yonder for a moment,' and raising my eyes, I saw the golden glory of the gods. We were at the boundary between the third and the fourth planes of being, where an electric, silvery, blue light faded into a golden yellow light, softer and more beautiful than can be described; since words fail to express the depth of feeling that was awakened at the sight of the scene that lay before me. But in that sacred moment it became pictured upon my memory, never to be effaced.

"There were Beings upon that plane who shone as brightly as the sun, and the colors that radiated from them were more beautiful than are those of a rainbow, because they were living, throbbing colors. And there was a soft melody in the air that seemed to come from every direction. There was a fragrance, too, so subtile and so sweet that it seemed to permeate everything. This perfume, I understood, was the essence or the souls of the flowers with which the land was filled.

" 'Is this the theologians' heaven, the place which they describe as the city with pearly gates and golden streets?' I asked my Master, and he replied:

" 'No. That plane is still beyond this one. I would show it to you, but you could not bear the vibrations of that realm. That plane is what the Eastern stu-

dents call Nirvana and is where perfected souls go to
rest forever and forever, as men reckon time. But
individual bliss in Nirvana does not last forever, since
all individual conditions must sometime change. The
egos who enter Nirvana have reached Godhood, and,
before leaving the fourth plane they elect whether
they will undertake the mission of assisting human
souls onward in their development or pass into Nir-
vanic bliss and finally fade out as individual souls
and be absorbed into the yellow cosmic current, becoming a part of the universal spiritual force.[1] Many
choose to become one with that force and forever lose
their individuality rather than return to earth and
witness the sinning and suffering there. Others, after
reaching this plane, and after resting here for a season prefer to return to earth and assist those who are
coming on behind. " 'Then those Beings return to the
world's battle ground where they sometimes incarnate
as Saviours or Avatars and lead such egos as will be
led out of the bondage of ignorance and into a knowledge of truth, which is freedom.

" 'The ancient religious teachers, as you now understand, selected the two extreme conditions or states
of consciousness as heaven and hell, and omitted the
intermediate planes of being, except the first subjective plane, which they call purgatory, where the
majority of disembodied souls go. By working upon
man's fears and hopes they expected to prevent his

---

[1] The History and Power of Mind, pp. 132, 133, 138, 157, 158, 224, 237.
From Incarnation to Re-incarnation, pp. 138-139.

sinning and thus raise him to higher realms. They did what they thought best at the different periods of time in which they served humanity. But old forms and old systems of religion must give way to new, and man now needs greater truths and more freedom of thought than ever before during this period of evolution.' "

THE END.

INDEX

Featured Titles from Westphalia Press

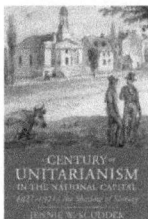

A Century of Unitarianism in the National Capital, 1821-1921
by Jennie W. Scudder

Jennie Scudder's work traces the sometimes controversial history of Unitarianism in the District of Columbia, centering on All Souls Unitarian Church. The account includes the development in the District and surrounding towns in northern Virginia and Southern Maryland.

The Rise of the Book Plate: An Exemplative of the Art
by W. G. Bowdoin, Introduction by Henry Blackwel

Bookplates were made to denote ownership and hopefully steer the volume back to the rightful shelf if borrowed. They often contained highly stylized writing, drawings, coat of arms, badges or other images of interest to the owner.

The Great Indian Religions
by G. T. Bettany

G. T. (George Thomas) Bettany (1850-1891) was born and educated in England, attending Gonville and Caius College in Cambridge University, studying medicine and the natural sciences. This book is his account of Brahmanism, Hinduism, Buddhism, and Zoroastrianism

Unworkable Conservatism: Small Government, Free-markets, and Impracticality by Max J. Skidmore

Unworkable Conservatism looks at what passes these days for "conservative" principles—small government, low taxes, minimal regulation—and demonstrates that they are not feasible under modern conditions.

Secrets & Lies in the United Kingdom: Analysis of Political Corruption
Edited by by Fabienne Portier-Le Cocq

Secrets & Lies in the United Kingdom: Analysis of Political Corruption lifts the shroud of secrecy in the United Kingdom in relation to modern freemasonry in Scotland in the late-18th century, the 'Stolen Generations' in Australia from the early 1900s to the late 1970s, and so much more.

Boston Unitarianism 1820-1850
by Octavius Brooks Frothingham

From the author, "Many years ago I proposed writing something in memory of Dr. Frothingham, but abandoned the project on account of the meagerness of the biographical material. Within the twelvemonth, a warm friend and admirer of his asked me to prepare a memoir."

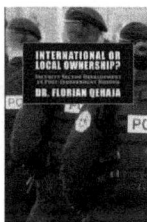

International or Local Ownership?: Security Sector Development in Post-Independent Kosovo
by Dr. Florian Qehaja

International or Local Ownership? contributes to the debate on the concept of local ownership in post-conflict settings, and discussions on international relations, peacebuilding, security and development studies.

The Bahai Movement: A Series of Nineteen Papers
by Charles Mason Remey

Charles Mason Remey (1874-1974) was the son of Admiral George Collier Remey and grew up in Washington DC. He studied to be an architect at Cornell (1893-1896) and the Ecole des Beaux Arts in Paris (1896-1903), where he learned about the Baha'i faith, and quickly adopted it.

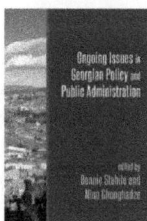

Ongoing Issues in Georgian Policy and Public Administration
Edited by Bonnie Stabile and Nino Ghonghadze

Thriving democracy and representative government depend upon a well functioning civil service, rich civic life and economic success. Georgia has been considered a top performer among countries in South Eastern Europe seeking to establish themselves in the post-Soviet era.

Poverty in America: Urban and Rural Inequality and Deprivation in the 21st Century
Edited by Max J. Skidmore

Poverty in America too often goes unnoticed, and disregarded. This perhaps results from America's general level of prosperity along with a fairly widespread notion that conditions inevitably are better in the USA than elsewhere. Political rhetoric frequently enforces such an erroneous notion.